MAY 1 9 2016

3 1994 01547 6887

SANTA ANA PUBLIC LIBRARY

D0821562

the

great

clod

Books by Gary Snyder

POETRY

Riprap and Cold Mountain Poems

Myths and Texts

The Back Country

Regarding Wave

Turtle Island

Axe Handles

Left Out in the Rain

No Nature

Mountains and Rivers Without End

This Present Moment

PROSE

Earth House Hold

He Who Hunted Birds in His Father's Village

Passage Through India

The Real Work

The Practice of the Wild

A Place in Space

The Gary Snyder Reader

Back on the Fire

The High Sierra of California (with Tom Killion)

Tamalpais Walking (with Tom Killion)

The Selected Letters of Allen Ginsberg and Gary Snyder

Distant Neighbors: The Selected Letters of Wendell Berry and Gary Snyder

304.2 SNY
Snyder, Gary
The great clod

$25.00
CENTRAL 31994015476887

GREAT CLOD

notes and memoirs on

nature and history in east asia

GARY SNYDER

COUNTERPOINT

Copyright © 2016 by Gary Snyder

All rights reserved under International and Pan-American Copyright Conventions. No part of this book may be used or reproduced in any manner whatsoever without written permission from the publisher, except in the case of brief quotations embodied in critical articles and reviews.

Library of Congress Cataloging-in-Publication Data is available
ISBN 978-1-61902-569-1

Cover design by Kelly Winton
Cover art by Yoshiaki Shimizu
Interior design by David Bullen

C O U N T E R P O I N T
2560 Ninth Street, Suite 318
Berkeley, CA 94710
www.counterpointpress.com

Printed in the United States of America
Distributed by Publishers Group West

10 9 8 7 6 5 4 3 2 1

to Burton Watson

Contents

The Great Clod burdens me with form, labors me with life, eases me in old age, and rests me in death. So if I think well of my life, for the same reason I must think well of my death.

Chuang-tzu

Introduction

In 1969 I had just recently returned to the west coast from a long residence in Japan. Fully ready to move out to the forests and mountains of the west, I was a bit surprised — over lunch one day — when David Brower of the newly minted "Earth Island Institute" proposed that I go back to Japan, specifically the northern island of Hokkaido. He wanted me to write a piece on the environmental issues of the island and its remaining indigenous peoples, known as Ainu. He proposed that I travel together with a photographer, saying that the finished article would then be used to enlarge people's understanding of the island and possibly help the world resist the development of a Winter Olympics plan that had come up for the Sapporo area. What he really wanted was ammunition against the proposed Olympics.

Though I'd been in Japan over ten years I'd never gotten to Hokkaido. I had climbed and hiked through the high mountains of Honshu, been out on the north coast and on southern island live volcanoes but not to the woodsy north. I'd studied up on the indigenous peoples,

the "Ainu," and knew something of the Hokkaido Brown
Bear, an *Ursus Arctos* cousin of the North American Griz.
So I was drawn to learn more, though I never had paid
much attention to the Olympic Games.

In 1971, having just finished building a little house in
the northern Sierra—and moved in, books, tools, and
family—thus somewhat able to take off for a couple of
months, I decided to do it. He introduced me to photographer Franz Berko. We made our plans. Brower
promised to cover the air fare and travel expenses, and
eventually pay a little share to Berko and me. Once back
in the Sierra I went to work putting up an extra winter's firewood and other useful chores. I pored over maps
and located a copy of Kindaichi's volume on Ainu oral
literature and tracked down Brown Bear stories—my
own particular fascination. Our time in Hokkaido was
scheduled for the coming summer of 1972.

In June of 1972 I went to the UN Conference on the
Environment in Stockholm (courtesy of Stewart Brand
and the Whole Earth Catalog), and then directly on to
Tokyo in July where I rendezvoused with Berko. We got
ourselves up to Sapporo by train, rented a Mitsubishi 4wd
suv, and headed into the interior.

This book is not the story of time in Hokkaido, though;
that comes later. Travel and hike we did—Berko took

a quantity of photos—and in mid-August we returned to North America. Months went by and then years, but I was never able to herd my information and ideas into a coherent account and the hoped-for article was never written. I was a disappointment to Brower and Berko both. I was new to the practice of prose-writing, and imagined myself able to accomplish large things.

Also I came to think that to write something about Hokkaido I would have to get a better grasp on Japanese environmental history, and for that I'd have to understand what had happened over 2,500 years of China. But there wasn't much, then, on Chinese environmental history. I searched libraries in Northern California and ordered up learned articles by mail as best I could.

Later my wife Masa and I were part of a group of American writers that was invited to the Chinese Mainland to meet writers and students in 1984. Around the same time I made several more trips to Japan and learned my way around farming, fishing, and carpentry with counterculture Japanese friends. Mark Elvin's groundbreaking book *The Retreat of the Elephants* came out, and Vaclav Smil's work on contemporary Chinese environmental problems. I began to think that all my research and writing was too late and too eccentric to be of use.

I had my own sort of skewed nature-loving fanaticism

as a boy, and I don't know where it came from. The big stumps of the original douglas fir and western hemlock forest of the Puget Sound region surrounded my childhood dairy farm. The forest I grew up with was huge stumps, small new firs and cedars, dense shrubby trees like cascara and vine maple, a few wild hazels, and a forest floor of salmonberries, oregon grape, salal, and native wild blackberries. I regularly climbed up and high onto a large old western red cedar that was not far from the back fence-line of our cow pasture. How did I become such an animist someone once asked me and I said I think I was radicalized by the ghosts of the original trees still hanging out by their stumps and telling me what had gone on. At any rate I was dubious about the direction the American dream seemed to be heading, building further new houses everywhere, and so I was open to other views, such as the idea that non-human beings were worthy of moral regard. Then I was exposed to East Asian paintings at the Seattle Art Museum and a bit later as a college undergraduate was reading Confucius and Lao-tzu and Chuang-tzu (as well as the Homeric epics and Greek drama and much else). I remember distinctly the time it came to me that perhaps China and Japan were fully developed high humanistic civilizations that had made peace with nature! I didn't let go of that idea for years.

Over a dinner once our friend Will Hearst asked me what had gotten me interested in China while still a youth. I surprised myself by saying right out "I got interested at an early age in East Asia. But for the wrong reasons." The conversation kept moving so swiftly that no one came back to asking what the "wrong reasons" were, but I didn't forget that I had said that. It reflected the surprise I felt during my first several years living in Japan when I came to see that the landscape was thoroughly used and worn, and that the signs of human obliviousness to the wild were everywhere. Plantation-style small conifer forests alternating with recent clearcuts in the hills, farmyards without an inch of land let be, cement blocks and rocks thrown into every stream-bank. I began the process of measuring the condition of the land itself against the written literature and transmitted accounts.

Nothing remarkable about that. Every time and place tells itself the stories it wants to hear. There's a sharp little haiku that goes "Even in Kyoto . . . I'm nostalgic for Kyoto."

Later visiting South Korea and Taiwan, as well as the mainland zones of both the Ho and the Chiang — the Yellow River and the Yangtze — I saw the varying degrees of use and impact everywhere. And a few almost pristine little jungles and groves tucked in here and there. That, combined with reading Burton Watson's translation of the *Histories* of Ssu-ma Ch'ien, "China's first historian," woke me up to the remarkable energy and drive of the East Asian peoples, whose art and poetry—or Daoist, Confucian, and Buddhist ethics—are but one small aspect of a fiercely normal chunk of humanity, that still considers itself to be the prime tribe of all, destined to lead the world. If those early Chinese social and natural thinkers were so precise and clear, it must have been that they deeply intuited the dangers that lay ahead—huge population and remarkably centralized power.

"I got interested in China for the wrong reasons." That is, I thought I had come onto a fully engaged civilization that maintained a respectful and careful regard for the land itself, and the many other beings who already lived there. It turned out that I was wrong, but in a very complex and challenging way.

GS 27. XII 15

THE
GREAT
CLOD

Summer in Hokkaido

For some years I lived in Japan, in the old capital of Kyoto. I had come to study Buddhism, but I couldn't break myself of walking in the forests and mountains and learning the names and habits of birds, animals, and plants. I also got to know a little about the farmers, the carpenters, and the fishermen; and the way they saw the mountains and rivers of their land. From them I learned there were deep feelings about the land that went below, and from before, the teachings of Buddhism. I was drawn to worship from time to time at Shinto shrines—at the foot of a mountain; by a waterfall; where two rivers come together; at the headwaters of a drainage. Doing this made me feel more at home in Japan, and for the first time I could relate to the forests of sugi and hinoki and pine almost as well as I could to the fir forest of my native Pacific Northwest. In other ways this drawing near to the gods of the earth and waters of Japan only added to my confusion. I was witnessing the accelerating modern Japanese economy, and the incredible transformation of the life of the people, and the landscape that this brought.

I had just begun to absorb the deep sense of place and reverence for the forces of nature this fine old civilization had maintained, to see it then turn and begin to devour itself. My literary peers, the avant-garde poets and artists of Tokyo, had no concern for either nature or the Buddha's teaching; but our minds met when we talked of the exploitation of the People, and sang radical folksongs. The young monks and laymen I meditated with in the temples of Kyoto were marvelous students of Buddhism and true bearers of the fine old manners of earlier Japan, but their sense of nature was restricted to tiny gardens, and they did not wish to speak about the exploitation of the masses at all. When I finally did, by good chance, meet a man I could speak with, about these things, he was neither a monk nor a marxist, but a propertyless vagabond Japanese Air Force veteran of World War II who spent his life walking with the mountains and rivers and farmers and working people of Japan.

We soon realized the questions we were raising about nature, human nature, and Far Eastern civilization have ramifications on a planetary scale. Here I have limited myself to working through the Buddhist teachings, the pre-Buddhist almost universal "old ways," the information of history, and my own experience of the natural world. Working in this book, with the question, how did the old civilization of Japan end up becoming so resolutely growth and profit oriented? There will be no answer here, but there will be many angles of vision and something about civilization and ourselves. I was with this question that I found myself, one midsummer, in Sapporo, a city of over a million with wide straight streets — in Hokkaido — the northernmost island of Japan; the one place still considered somewhat wild.

The first time I had set foot in Japan was almost twenty years before, straight off the ship *Arita Mara*; two weeks churning across the Pacific watching the Laysan Albatrosses weave back and forth in its wake. There was a truckload of caged seals on the way through Customs in Kobe, snaking their small heads about. What I saw was the tightness of space: the crowded narrow-gauge commuter train, tens of thousands of tiny tile-roof houses along the track, little patches of vegetable gardens that shake every twenty minutes with the Special Express. Living then in Kyoto, I saw Hokkaido as the picture of cows and silo on a cheese box; I heard it was a sub-arctic wilderness, and my Japanese friends said "it's a lot like America," so for years I never went there. Will Petersen had been stationed as a soldier up north after the war; he loved it, he raved about the beautiful walls of snow the trains ran through, like tunnels, in the dead of winter.

But now it's summer in Hokkaido and really hot and I'm going through the swinging glass doors of the four-teen story Hokkaido circuit-government office building, into the wide lobby with elevators at several ends and sides. Across two walls, taking a right angle bend, is a mural. About eighty feet long, low relief on stone, "Hok-kaido's hundred years." It starts, as such murals do, with a native person sailing a little boat through great waves; with woods and deer; and then come the early explorers. It goes on to axe men, toppling trees and stumps; then expert advisors arriving on horses (these happened to be Americans), and soon there's an agricultural experiment station, cows and sheep, a college with a clock tower, a city laid out, a brewery, a pulp mill, a railroad train, and finally—men with air hammers blasting rocks.

One hundred years: since Japan moved in with finality and authority to this island—one fifth the size of all the rest of the country—and decided to leave it no longer to hunters and fisherfolk but to "put it to work" economically.

Through the ground floor lobby, across the back street and down the block is the entrance to the Botanical Gar-dens, where I am to meet Dr. Misao Tatewaki, a little mustache, big open smile, ponderous walk, suspenders. A large, handsome, friendly, dignified old man. He takes me upstairs in the wood-frame office building of the gardens, a semi-occidental 19th-century house with creaky stairs and fluttering curtains, to an empty meeting-room with an oiled plank floor. At the head of the stairs on the wall is an oil portrait of a Japanese gentleman in the high collar of the Victorian era. Dr. Tatewaki stopped and made a little bow. "Dr. Miyabe, my teacher of Botany," he says, and, "Dr. Miyabe was a disciple of Asa Gray." Lineages. Dr. Tatewaki asks for tea to be sent up. I open out two folding chairs and place them side by side at one end of the large table. I tell him only a little of what I hope to do and he leans back, sighs, looks at me and says, "Japan has a sickness. It is a sightseeing sickness. That means people don't come to see or learn of nature or beauty, but for fad." And he speaks long and sorrowfully of what has already happened to the mountains and forests of the main island of Honshu, and of what little hope he sees for Hokkaido.

So then we go for a stroll in the wild-looking garden, which is in part a swampy remnant of the original plant community in the heart of the city, with towering virgin birch and elm. "Sapporo" from the Ainu, meaning "Large Plain."

Later I meet Dr. Tatewaki at his office in the dark cement corridors of the building of the Faculty of

Agriculture at Hokkaido University. Books to the ceiling, books in heaps. Cases of boxes of color slides of plants. Hulten, *Arctic Flora*, Kihara's three volumes on Nepal, the U.S.F.S. *Atlas of U.S. Trees*, an old Shanghai Commercial Press book on forestry in China . . . Russian books . . . and he shows me the famous study, *Crabs of Sagami Bay* by the Showa Emperor himself, with superb color plates. Dr. Toyama, his former student, shows slides and Dr. Tatewaki names off the bushes and plants in Latin. "Those scholars in Tokyo don't understand the actual state of Hokkaido, they think it's one with maritime Siberia and east Manchuria . . . it's right in between warm-temperate Japan and the Siberian sub-arctic . . ."

Age nineteen, he came north hoping to study the plants of Sakhalin and the Kuriles. He has been here ever since. And browsing about the bookshelves, I find a little book of poems by Dr. Tatewaki, published in the late twenties. They are *w a k a*, the thirty-one-syllable poetic form one size up from haiku. The collection is called *Oka*, "hill" — and there's one on the Siberian people called Gilyaks who had a settlement in Hokkaido:

> "The misery of the Gilyaks
>   and the Gilyaks — not knowing their misery —
> today they laugh"

All He Sees Is Blue: Basic Far East

When the P'eng bird journeys to the southern darkness the waters are roiled for three thousand li. He beats the whirlwind and rises ninety thousand lim setting off on the sixth-month gale. Wavering heat, bits of dust, living things blowing each other about — the sky looks very blue. Is that its real color, or is it because it is so far away and has no end? When the bird looks down, all he sees is blue too.

CHUANG-TZU

I guess Dr. Tatewaki must have run into Gilyak people in Sakhalin; or perhaps the little colony in Abashiri on Hokkaido; I never asked him. This corner of the world; this place to live. Another human habitat. Eastern Manchuria, Maritime Siberia, North China drainages of the China Sea, Sakhalin, the Kuriles out as far as the end of Kamchatka, all the Japanese islands and the Ryukyus. The whole area, if you go by the grids on maps, roughly between 25 degrees and 50 degrees of latitude, 110 degrees to 160 degrees longitude. All of it more southerly than it *feels*: Hokkaido itself, in latitude, is level with Oregon. The Ryukyus will take you through Mexico and Bombay. Straight through the globe you'd find yourself somewhere around the Rio Grand Rise and the Argentine Basin, on the bottom of the South Atlantic, east of Uruguay and Argentina.

Tenki, the Japanese word for weather, means spirit/ breath/energy: of Heaven. You don't see the stars so much in this part of the world, there's a swirl of cloud mist-moisture always going. Before I went to Asia, I had heard that Japan would be like the Pacific Northwest. Northwest Pacific is not like Pacific Northwest, and the difference most obvious is summer rains, warm slow drizzles through June, sharp cooler downpours in July and August with some thunderstorms; windy typhoon-carried rains in September. Summer rains make for wet-rice agriculture, bamboo, and a different forest. It means that grasses have a harder time, with a great scramble of weeds and vines every spring, so that natural pastureland is scarce, only found in northern Japan uplands and in SE Hokkaido.

The coast of Asia and these offshore islands is the playground of ocean and continent forces that spiral and swirl—a *yin* and *yang* dance of cold and warm, wet and dry. Through the winter months the cold polar-continental air masses, "Siberian Air," centered over Lake Baikal, send dry chilly winds toward the oceans, giving the west side of the Japanese islands colder temperatures, clouds, and heavy snows. In late spring, moist air from the Okhotsk Sea brings the "plum rain" month of drizzles, with mould on the books, rust on the sewing needles, and soggy tobacco. Most of the rest of the summer "Ogasawara Air" from the Pacific streams northwest, sliding along tropical continental fronts, and culminating in whiplashes of typhoons in late August and September. Hokkaido gets less "plum rain" and fewer typhoons; much colder air in winter. Though not so far north as most of Europe, on the east side of Eurasia it has a climate like the maritime provinces of Canada, or New England.

Japan as a whole doesn't have as many thunderstorms as the American Southeast, but what it gets is strong—especially the winter storms. Only about 1 percent of all lightning bolts in the world are superbolts, which release 1 trillion watts of visible energy in 1/1000 of a second. Winter storms over Japan get considerably more than their share of globally observed superbolts. Some sort of dragons abound.

From the bottom up, too, energy and tension. The islands rise from a deep ocean—as much as seven miles from the top to bottom. (The average depth of the Pacific is two and a half miles.) The Ramapo Deep to the east is 34,448 feet. Even the Japan Sea, between Japan and the continent, is over 10,000 feet deep in spots. Five hundred volcanoes, with sixty eruptions known to history. Arcs and nodes of mountains: Hokkaido has at its center a rolling mass of mountains called Daisetsu, "Great Snowy Mountains," and this is the node of three arcs: one down from Saghalien, another arc which is the anchor point of the Kurile Islands, and a third arc which connects south with the mountains of Honshu.

Around these islands, and along the Asian coast, a system of currents is also swirling. The warm Kuroshio, Black Current (or "black tide") flowing north from near Taiwan, splits and the west part, Tsushima Current, flows on north through the Japan Sea and east through Tsugaru Strait between Honshu and Hokkaido; both branches meet the cold Oyashio, or Kurile current, moving down from the northeast, and at about latitude 38 degrees it slides below the warm current and weaves its way on south, undersea. The warm current, Kuroshio, is clear and salty, not so nutritious, indigo-blue. Tuna (maguro) and bonito (katsuo) ride with this current — the bonito loves water with 20 m transparency, not below 18 degrees C. The Japanese anchovy *(katakuchi iwashi)* and

Pacific sardine *(iwashi)* are also found in the Kuroshio. The Oyashio is rich in phosphates and full of plankton, and greenish-blue. The cold current gives eastern Hokkaido and Honshu coasts their fog and cold summers. Pacific herring *(nishui),* Pacific cod *(tara)*, *masu* salmon, and especially the mackerel pike, *sanma,* follow the cold current. The meeting place — interface — current rip — is off the island of Kinka-san on the NE coast of Honshu. It's a rich and famous fishing ground.

For most of Japan rain averages more than sixty inches a year. Hokkaido gets between forty and forty-five, with less in the area northeast of the Daisetsu mountains, the side facing toward the Okhotsh Sea.

Temperatures, and the amounts and patterns of rainfall, watershed by watershed, from sea-level to headwaters, make up the main terms that plants, animals, and finally humans respond to. Establish, first, the conditions of the plant communities: and everything flows from that. Temperature: the cherry comes into bloom when average daytime temperature reaches 50 degrees F. Thus blooming in Kyushu in late March, Tokyo in early April, Hokkaido in mid-May.

The realm of life is this place where air and ground, air and ocean surface meet, and down some depths more into the water. Living beings are down into the soil a yard or so, and into caves or cracks wherever water goes, and up into the sky as high as spiders ride on threads. On snowfields in the highest mountains are populations of mites that feed entirely on wind-blown pollen. A Bar-headed goose was once seen flying over the summit of Mt. Everest.

Great areas of Asia, particularly lowland China, no longer have their original/potential natural vegetation, and are missing much of their original fauna, but *what was* and *what might be* are still the basic terms of even human life in a place. Take away the farmers and the woodcutters and in a few centuries those excellently adapted beings, the life-forms of, say, the Yellow River Basin, will come back, ultimately to a climax forest. Not that in actual fact it will be exactly what it was three thousand years ago for some soils have moved away and some hills eroded bare. But given the chance, the forest will reconstitute.

The hills and valleys of the Pacific drainages of East Asia and the string of islands on the continental shelf were covered with a diverse and extensive forest. It was a direct descendant of Miocene plant communities, having undergone virtually no ice-age disturbance. Thus it had many affinities with the great hardwood forests of eastern North America (Great Smoky National Park).

South China and Japan (southwest of Tokyo) were an evergreen broadleaf forest of laurels, evergreen oaks, and other trees with hard glossy leaves. The Yangtze basin, central Japan, and most of Korea were a broadleaf deciduous forest. In the Yellow River lowlands this forest became predominantly oak. The mixed hardwood forest of Northeast Manchuria, north Korea and southwest Hokkaido (maple, tulip-tree, birch, and walnut slightly dominant out of forty or so commonly found species) gave way to conifer forests in the higher elevations and to the north. The Daisetsu mountains of Hokkaido are a rainfall line, and the beginning of a boreal coniferous forest, or taiga that covers the rest of the island. A taiga flourishes where the annual average temperature is below 43 degrees.

At the peak of the Würm glaciation, about 45,000 years ago, sea level was much lower and Hokkaido was simply part of Siberia; the land bridge eastward to Alaska was a thousand miles wide. Southern Japan was connected to China, via what is now the shallow Yellow Sea. Glaciers themselves were not so vast, just a few touches in the highest mountains. Glacial traces can be seen in the Hidaka range of Hokkaido, but ice was mainly in Siberia in the mountains north of the Lena River. The land bridge to the New World was ice-free and relatively level. Taiga

and steppe moved south a few hundred miles and East
Asia was if anything more hospitable to paleolithic hunters than Europe at the same time. In the final glaciation,
about 18,000 years ago, Hokkaido was again connected
with Siberia, and southwestern Japan was separated from
Korea by about twenty miles of water. Human beings
moved in at this time, if not before. The oldest known site
in Hokkaido is 20,000 years old; Japan about the same.
We don't have more and earlier sites and human remains
probably because the people and their homes along the
coast and at the mouths of rivers have been buried under
risen sea waters since the end of the last ice-age.

Across the plains of Northern Siberia and into the New
World came circumpolar hunters; and along the gentler
exposed coastal plains of glacial times, from the south,
came people of seas and rivers. The Japanese islands are
a meeting of maritime south and continental north, and
a westernmost meeting-point of techniques and styles
that are found around the whole North Pacific. From the
European standpoint, Hokkaido was a forgotten corner
of the world that finally Captain Cook sailed by; in planetary terms it is a pivot and crossroad of peoples as well as
climates, trees, and animals. Here's where the Arctic bear
meets the shorter-haired black bear of the south with the
white moon bib. And the Gilyak, a paleo-Asiatic people of
the Siberian Amur Coast, also called Nivkhi (a Mongol-

oid people who wore conical birchbark hats and provided Marxist anthropologists with what they thought was one clear case of Group Marriage).

The Gilyaks had a delicious raw-fish-with-wild-garlic-salad; sometimes trading-friends, sometimes enemies, of their neighbors the Ainu.

The whole of Japan today is a population of around 127,000,000. Hokkaido, about the size of Ireland, has 5,255,000 people, of which 25,000 are considered Ainu. Mr. Tawara of the Nature Protection Agency, over tea in his office upstairs in the Hokkaido Circuit Government Building, told me there are still about three thousand *Ursus Arctos* in Hokkaido, big as grizzlies, too — not bad, when you consider that wild bears became extinct in Britain in the 12th century AD.

The Great Clod: China and Nature

You hide your boat in the ravine and your fish net in the
swamp and tell yourself that they will be safe. But in the
middle of the night a strong man shoulders them and car-
ries them off, and in your stupidity you don't know why
it happened. You think you do right to hide little things
in big ones, and yet they get away from you. But if you
were to hide the world in the world, so that nothing could
get away, this would be the final reality of the constancy
of things.

CHUANG-TZU

The Cascades of Washington, and the Olympics, are wet, rugged, densely forested mountains that are hidden in cloud and mist much of the year. As they say around Puget Sound, "If you can see Mt. Rainier it means it's going to rain. If you can't see Mt. Rainier, that means it's raining." When I was a boy of nine or ten I was taken to the Seattle Art Museum and was struck more by Chinese landscape paintings than anything I'd seen before, and maybe since. I saw first that they looked like real mountains, and mountains of an order close to my heart; second that they were different mountains of another place and true to those mountains as well; and third that they were mountains of the spirit and that these paintings pierced into another reality which both was and was not the same reality as "the mountains."

That seed lodged in my store-house-consciousness to be watered later when I first read Arthur Waley's translations of Chinese poetry and then Ezra Pound's. I thought, here is a high civilization that has managed to keep in tune with nature. The philosophical and religious writings I later read from Chinese seemed to back this up. I even thought for a time that simply because China had not been Christian, and had been spared an ideology which separated humankind from all other living beings (with the two categories of redeemable and unredeemable) that it naturally had an organic, process-oriented view of the world. Japan and China have had indeed a uniquely appropriate view of the natural world, which has registered itself in many small, beautiful ways through history. But we find that large, civilized societies inevitably have a harsh effect on the natural environment, regardless of philosophical or religious values.

OSTRICH EGGS

The late Pleistocene was a rich time for the people of Asia. Great herds of mammals on the tundra and grasslands. The reindeer-herders of present-day Soviet Siberia come down in a direct line from the later ice age when reindeer was the major food of people across Eurasia. A few Tungusic reindeer herders are probably still there in the NW Khingan mountains of Manchuria, within China's present borders.

The early post-glacial warming trend changed tundra to forest. The dry lake beds of Mongolia ("nors" to our North American "playas") were wet then, and people making many microtools lived on their marshy margins. Their quarry was largely ostrich and ostrich eggs. Parts of North China which are barren now were densely forested with oaks, beeches, elms, ash, maple, catalpa, poplar, walnut, chestnut; and pines, firs, larch, cedar, spruce species—and much more.

At Lin-hsi in Jehol, Sha-kang in Hsin-min Hsien, Liaoning, and Ang-ang-hsi in Heilungchiang, cultural deposits were found in a black earth layer, which lies beneath a yellowish sandy layer of recent formation and above the loess deposits of Pleistocene origin. This black earth layer . . . probably represents an ancient forest cover.

The existence of a thick forest cover in North China and on the Manchurian plains is further indicated by cultural remains from prehistoric sites, such as the abundance of charcoal and woodworking implements (axe, adze, chisel, etc.) and by the frequency of bones of wild game. Some of these bones are definitely from forest-dwelling animals such as tigers and deer.

A little farther north, at Djailai-nor, in North China, implements of stone, bone, and antler, and willow basket-work have been found in direct association with remains of woolly rhinoceros, bison, and mammoth — an association of tools and animal remains also found in southern Manchurian sites.

At other North Chinese sites animal remains have been found that indicate it was a bit warmer in early recent times; Chang's list of species:

Bamboo rat
Elephant
Rhinoceros
Bison
Tapir
Water Buffalo
Water deer
Pere David's deer

Menzies' deer
Porcupine
Squirrel
Warmth-loving molluscs

Kwan-chih Chang thinks the woodland mesolithic of China is likely the forerunner of Neolithic agricultural settlements, and was in its time related to the Siberian paleolithic, the European mesolithic, and the woodland cultures of Japan and North America. This archaic internationalism has long been lost to China and civilized Japan, but for those who have eyes and ears it is still present in tiny spots in North America. The life of the Ainu on the island of Hokkaido was a continuation of that culture up until less than a century ago.

The mountains of Eastern Manchuria are still a refuge of the old forest. Dudley Stamp said (before World War II) that the forests of oak, ash, walnut, poplar, spruce, fir, and larch were largely untouched except near the railways. George Cressey, also writing in the thirties, says twenty to thirty thousand men were employed every winter logging the forest at the headwaters of the Manchurian Sungari River — floating the logs down to Kirin City — "and the forests are being rapidly destroyed with slight regard for the future."

"MILLET"

Civilized China has its roots in the Neolithic villages
along the Huang (Yellow) River Valley, especially at the
place where the Huang River takes a sharp turn north,
and the Wei and Lo and Fen Rivers join it. Millennia
of fishing, gathering, and hunting on the forest-river-
marsh margins—and here a slow steady domestication
of plants and animals; the emergence of weaving and
pottery. Settlements of the Yang-shou type, which are
dated as being between four and six thousand years old,
present us with an already accomplished painted hand-
turned pottery, round and square houses, and differenti-
ated kiln and cemetery sections of town. Yet agrarian
life is still interfaced with the wild: leopard, water deer,
wild cattle, deer, rhinoceros, bamboo rat, hare, marmot
and antelope bones are found in the middens, along with
stone and bone points. We find net-weights of pottery
or stone and bone harpoons and fishhooks. Chang lists
the characteristics of those autonomous, self-sufficient,
flourishing communities:

cultivated millet and rice; possibly kao-liang and soy-
bean; domesticated pigs, cattle, sheep, dogs, chickens,

possibly horses; tamped-earth and wattle-and-daub construction; white plastered walls; domesticated silkworms; weaving silk and hemp; pottery with cord or mat-impressed designs; pottery with three hollow legs; pottery steamers; crescent-shaped stone knives and rectangular cleaver-axe; jade and wood-carving.

These already-sophisticated, stable villages are witness to a way of life, in place, of great attention and care that antedates their archaeological dates by several thousand years. They are already by 4000 BC fine expressions of the possibilities of the Yellow River watershed bio-region; Anderson described burial sites on the Panshan Hills, twelve hundred feet above the village-sites along the T'ao River and a six-mile trip from the houses, where people had been carried and buried for countless decades, "resting places from which they could behold in a wide circle the place where they had grown up, worked, grown grey, and at last found a grave swept by the winds and bathed by sunshine."

To the east and along the coast, another pottery tradition, black and polished, took precedence about five thousand years ago—given the type-name Lung-shan. This culture pioneered and expanded both north and south from Shantung and the mouth of the Huang; and the mix of the several types that resulted is the full Chines Neolithic. The size and specializations of some of the later sites would seem to set the stage for an urban civilization.

Writing and Slaves

The first civilization is called the "Shang," basically the successful rule of one city-state over a number of other emerging city-states. It is dated from the middle of the second millennium BC. It is distinguished by bronze technology, writing, horse-and-chariot, a ruling class made up of several aristocratic warrior clans of luxurious ways, large numbers of apparent slaves as well as a very poor peasant class. These traits are all discontinuous with the Neolithic.

This is a great change in ways. How a free, untaxed, self-sustaining people can be made into a serf or slave populace, whose hard-earned surplus is taken by force to support a large class of non-producers, is perhaps the major question of history. It is, in fact, where "history" starts — not an auspicious beginning. We have some traces of how the people thought in that free time. There seems to have been bear worship, deer dances, festivals for mountains and rivers, festivals for the spirits of plants and great get-togethers for young lovers and musicians. We even have some songs surviving which may be close to the very songs they sang.

Part of the trick in corralling an energy supply beyond your own labor and skill is organization. Slavery is the fossil fuel of the second millennium; bronze the uranium. The invention of writing (analogous to the computer today) and a class of clerks provides the organizing pathways for re-channeling wealth away from its makers. In primitive society, surpluses are exchanged directly among groups or members of groups; peasants, however, are rural cultivators whose surpluses are transferred to a dominant group of rulers that uses the surpluses both to underwrite its own standard of living and to distribute the remainder to groups in society that do not farm but must be fed for their specific goods and services to turn. From that time, 1500 BC, the balance of man and nature, and the standard of living of the farming people of China, began to go down.

The rulers become persons who are alienated from direct contact with soil, growth, manure, sweat, craft — their own bodies' powers. The peasants become alienated from the very land they used to assume belonged to Mother Earth herself, and not to a Duke or King. Games

of social and political intrigue absorb the aristocrats—
"getting by" absorbs the farmers. The old religion of
gratitude, trust, and exchange with nature is eroded. The
state seeks only to maximize its stance, and it begins to
seem possible to get away with excessive exploitation of
nature itself, as the scene of impact is moved over the
hills, into the next watershed, out of sight. Gratitude is
channeled toward the Rulers in a state religion, and the
Mother-oriented Neolithic religion becomes "low-class"
or goes underground. The Shang rulers, in the intoxica-
tion of wealth and power, became profligate and turbulent to the point that even later Chinese history frowns.

It may be that the parallel between our own fossil fuel
era is apt—energy beyond imagining—"energy slaves"
available—throws a whole society off keel into excess,
confusion, and addiction.

The Shang made staggering use of its human energy
slaves. An estimate has been made of the work it took
to build the great earthen wall around the Shang city of
Cheng-chou:

The wall was roughly rectangular in shape, with a
total perimeter of 7195 meters and an enclosed area of
3.2 square km. The maximum height of the surviving
wall is 9.1 meters and the maximum width at the base

of the wall, 36 meters. The wall was built in successive compressed layers, each of which has an average thickness of 8 to 10 centimeters. On the surface of each layer are clear depressions made by the pestles used for compressing work, and the soil making up the wall is hard and compact. Chin-huai estimates the original wall to have been 10 meters in average height, with an average width of 20 meters, which, multiplied by the total length of 7195 meters, required no less than 1,439,000 meters cubed of compressed soil or (using a ratio of 1.2) 2,878,000 meters cubed of loose soil. Experiments carried out by archaeologists show that an average worker produced 0.03 meters cubed of earth by means of a bronze pick or 0.02 meters cubed by means of a stone hoe. He concludes that to build the whole city wall of Cheng-chou, including earth digging, transporting, and compressing, required no less than eighteen years, with ten thousand workers working three hundred and thirty days a year.

Civilization came to China, it seems, fifteen hundred years later than it did to the ancient near east. But the evidence shows that a neolithic economy and style begins as early in China as in the Occident. Thus China gets less civilization and more neolithic. Rather than taking that (as most do) as puzzling on the part of China, or a sign of western superiority, I think the opposite: by somehow staving off urbanization and class structure longer, Chinese culture was able to more fully incubate itself in the great strengths of Neolithic-type culture: village self-government networks, an adequate and equal material base, a round of festivals and ceremonies, and a deep grounding in the organic processes and cycles of the natural sphere. This accounts I think for the basic health and resilience of the Chinese people through all the trials of civilization since.

The *Shih Ching*, "Classic of Songs," was gathered up from the oral tradition and put in writing around the fifth century BC. It reflects a much larger and older song-lore. Many songs are clearly from the feudal circles of the Shang and Chou societies; but some are from the fields and hills, and in that way echo the people's archaic culture with its playfulness and sanity. Here's one, a girl's song—

> Gathering fennel
> gathering fennel,
> on top of Sunny Point,
> the stories people tell don't
> believe them at all
> let it be, let it be

it's not so at all the
stories people tell,
what could be gotten from them?

Gathering bitterleaf
gathering bitterleaf
under Sunny Point,
the stories people tell don't
pay them any mind
let it be, let it be
it's not so at all the
stories people tell,
what could be gotten from them?

Gathering wild carrot
gathering wild carrot
east of Sunny Point,
the stories people tell don't
go along with them
let it be, let it be
it's not so at all the
stories people tell,
what could be gotten from them?

The Way

The Shang dynasty dissipated around the beginning of the first millennium bc and was followed by the Chou. For five hundred years the Chou maintained itself as an increasingly divided federation of smaller states and then broke up completely. That next period is called "Warring States."

Civilized China had become two widely separated cultures—a patriarchal, militaristic, pragmatic network of related rulers and ruling families (that crossed the lines of the various Warring States), and a "common people" with a folk-culture rooted in a long healthy past and a strong measure of surviving village customary government. The bronze-age rulers even had a religion of their own (saying "The Rites do not go down to the common people"), which revolved around auguries and sacrifice. Auguries because a ruling house has a stake in the longer future just like a man with money in stocks suddenly starts figuring interest rates and worries about the economic "climate." Sacrifice, a curious perversion of food-chain sacramentalism, was offered largely to the legendary memories of the successful power-seizing clan forebears, fathers of the state, whom they thought of as "Ancestors in Heaven."

The rulers and scholars of fourth century bc China

were people obsessed by society and its problems. Out of
the literate class of record-keeping scribes, clerks, astrolo-
gers, and teachers, individuals emerged with ideas for
rectifying the social and political scene — or totally doing
away with it.

Some of these people come to us in history as "sages."
(Members of the oppressed class who thought similar
thoughts might be called "charismatic peasant prophets"
or "inflammatory female faith-healers" — or sometimes
they just drew back into the mountains to be woodcutter-
hermits. Later Chinese sages often aspired to be taken for
woodcutter-hermits.)

Actually, one philosophical set, the Legalists, were all
in favor of the State and argued only that rulers should
be more draconian and purge themselves of any concern
for the feelings of the common people.

Confucius and his school tried to mediate between the
arrogance of the aristocrats and the people they ruled by
teaching a philosophy of humanitarian government conducted by virtuous professionals. Much of Confucianism
is charming and sensible, but the tilt toward the State is
visible in it from the first.

Followers of Mo-tzu, a school little-known now but
strong in its time, seemed allied in form if not in spirit
with the common people. They wore coarse clothes,

ate coarse food, and labored incessantly, with a doctrine of universal love. Their feelings about the State were ambiguous—they believed in strong defensive warfare and rule by the virtuous.

And that brings us to the most striking world-view in the whole Far East and one of the world's top two or three: Philosophical Daoism. By what standard does one dare criticize a whole society?

One can criticize a society by measuring it against a set of religiously received values—as do say, the Amish or the Jehovah's Witnesses. Or, quite common in the world today, one can subscribe to an analysis of society and history which holds that there are better alternatives of a rational, humanitarian, and utilitarian order. (A truly "scientific" critique of a society would have to draw on the information we are now gathering worldwide from anthropology, ecology, psychology, and whatnot—and that study is still in its infancy.)

The ancient mystics—artisans and thinkers now called "Daoists"—sought a base of value in the observable order of nature and its intuitable analogs in human nature. The size of Mind this gave them, and their irreverent, witty, gentle, accurate insights still crackle in the world today. The key texts are the *Dao-de Jhing*, and the texts called *Chang-tzu* and *Lieh-tzu*.

Dao is translated path, or way, the way things are, the way beyond a "way." They were social visionaries, naturalists, and mystics, living in a China still rich with wild-life and upland forest.

The Daoist social position invokes a pre-civilized, Mother-oriented world which once existed, and could exist again:

I have heard that in ancient times the birds and beasts were many and the people few . . . people all nested in trees in order to escape danger, during the day gathering acorns and chestnuts, at sundown climbing back up to sleep in their trees. Hence they were called the people of the Nestbuilder. In ancient times the people knew nothing about wearing clothes. In summer they heaped up great piles of firewood, in winter they burned them to keep warm. Hence they were called 'the people who know how to stay alive.' In the age of Shen Nung, the people lay down peaceful and easy, woke up wide-eyed and blank. They knew their mothers but not their fathers, and lived side by side with the elk and the deer. They plowed for food, wove their clothing, and had no thought in their hearts of harming one another. This was Perfect Virtue at its height!

Following Marcel Granet and other scholars it seems the case that Neolithic Chinese society was indeed matrilineal and matrilocal, with a large share of religious life conducted by the *wu*, shamans — largely female.

Confucianists declined to look closely at nature. Daoists were not only good observers, but rose above human-centered utilitarianism, as in this story from Lieh-tzu:

> Mr. T'ien, of the State of Ch'i, was holding an ancestral banquet in his hall, to which a thousand guests had been invited. As he sat in their midst, many came up to him with presents of fish and game. Eyeing them approvingly, he exclaimed with unction, 'How generous is Heaven to man! Heaven makes the five kinds of grain to grow, and brings forth the finny and the feathered tribes, especially for our benefit.' All Mr. Tien's guests applauded this sentiment to the echo, except the twelve-year-old son of a Mr. Pao, who, regardless of seniority, came forward and said, 'It is not as my Lord says. The ten thousand creatures in the universe and we ourselves belong to the same category, that of living things, and in this category there is nothing noble or nothing mean. It is only by reason of size, strength, or cunning, that one particular species gains the mastery over another, or that one feeds upon another. None

of them are produced in order to subserve the uses of others. Man catches and eats those that are fit for his food, but how could it be said that Heaven produced them just for him? Mosquitoes and gnats suck blood through human skin, tigers and wolves devour human flesh but we do not thereby assert that Heaven produced man for the benefit of mosquitoes and gnats, or to provide food for tigers and wolves.'

In pursuing their study of nature ("nature" in Chinese is tzu-jan, self-so, self-thus, that which is self-maintaining and spontaneous) into human nature and the dark interior of phenomena, the Daoist writers stress softness, ignorance, the flow, a wise receptivity; silence. They bring forward a critical paradox; namely, thermal physical energy flows into unavailability and is lost apparently forever: entropy. Life appears to be an intricate strategy to delay and make use of this flow. But what might be called "spiritual" energy often grows in strength only when you "let go" — give up — "cast off body and mind" — become one with the process. The Lao Tzu text says,

> The Valley Spirit never dies.
> It is called the Mysterious Female.
> The gate of the Mysterious Female

Is the beginning of Heaven and Earth.
It's always there —
No matter how much you draw on it —
It will never be exhausted.

Dao-de Jhing, Chapter 6

This principle is the key to understanding Daoism. Do nothing against the flow, and all things are accomplished. Daoists taught that human affairs as well as the systems and sub-systems move smoothly of their own accord; and that all order comes from within, all the parts, and that the notion of a need for a centralized ruler, Divine or Political, is a snare.

How then did mankind lose the way? The Daoists can only answer, through meddling, through doubt, through some error. And, it can't really be lost. The Ch'an (Zen) Buddhists centuries later addressed this with typical paradoxical energy: "The Perfect Way is without difficulty: strive hard!" China has been striving all these centuries.

THE HOUSE OF LIFE

Another way of seeing nature, out of the south (the old pre-Han state of Ch'u), is in a body of poems that echoes a culture open to vision and communication with the non-human realms, using a rich language of Yangtze valley vegetation. These poems—Ch'u Tz'u, "Words of Ch'u"—include the elegant "Nine Songs" of young girl—or young man—dance and spirit-calling trance. They are in Chinese official history almost by accident. Literate persons, Ch'u Yüan himself perhaps, re-wrote songs heard at folk festivals and they entered the canon as political allegories. The "Mountain Goddess" is described as

> Driving tawny leopards, leading the striped lynxes;
>   A carriage of lily-magnolia with banner of
>   woven cassia;
> Her cloak of stone-orchids, her belt of asarum:
> She gathers sweet scents to give to the one she loves.

The shrines or temples or glades used for this worship were called "House of Life."

SALT AND IRON

Government monopolies on salt and iron and alcohol for revenue; huge public works projects; the draining of marshes and thousands of miles of canals built by conscript labor. Though Daoism was granted a certain prestige that rose and fell with different periods of history, the work of an expanding civilization and its dedicated, orderly administrators, was the real line of force.

Ssu-ma Ch'ien, the great historian, writes on canals, second century BC, early Han dynasty —

> . . . the emperor Wu Ti ordered Hsi Po, a water engineer from Ch'i, to plot the course of the transport canal, and called up a force of twenty or thirty thousand laborers to do the digging. After three years of labor it was opened for use in hauling grain and proved to be extremely beneficial. From this time on grain transport to the capital gradually increased, while people living along the canal were able to make considerable use of the water to irrigate their fields.

Emperor Wu's regime employed Legalist Party advisors: the People were stretched close to breaking. Even Confucian critics, though heard, were ridiculed.

81 BC, a high official answered their debates —

> See them now present us with nothingness and consider it substance, with emptiness and call it plenty! In their coarse gowns and cheap sandals they walk gravely along sunk in meditation as though they had

lost something. These are not men who can do great deeds and win fame. They do not even rise above the vulgar masses!

The Han dynasty had succeeded the Ch'in — 3rd century BC — brutal and short-lived — which unified the Warring States. For four hundred years Han rulers maintained a centralized, imperial nation that at its farthest reach made trading contact with Rome. It broke apart, like the Chou, into competing smaller powers and states.

"Wild" in China

The people of mainstream China call themselves *"Han"* people, even today. The term is contrasted with any and all "ethnic" groupings—such as the people of the south known as the *Yüeh* (modern *Viet* of Vietnam), who "cut their hair short and tattooed themselves."

Even in the fourth century AD we can assume that the forests and agriculturally marginal areas of greater China were inhabited, even if thinly, by either backwoods Han people or tribal people.

The post-Han "Six Dynasties" period witnessed a flourishing back-to-nature movement from within the ruling gentry class, a "nature" that extended from the fields and gardens of the suburbs to the really deep hills. Many people who might in less turbulent times have exercised their class prerogative of administrative employment turned away toward an idea of purity and simplicity. Not all were wealthy or self-indulgent. The poet T'ao Yuan-ming (T'ao Ch'ien) (365–427) was a very minor official, whose early retirement to a small farm was his own choice. His poems are still the classic standard of a certain quietness, openness, emptiness, and also human frankness and frailty in the confusions of farm, family, and wine, that much later Chinese poetry aspires to. The Daoist idea of being nobody in the world, "behind instead of in front" gave strength to those who often must have missed the social life of their urban *literati* friends, as they sat up late reading and drinking alone in their estates or in homesteads out amongst the peasants.

Some of the Han dynasty poems picture wild mountain scenery as scary and horrible. As Burton Watson points out, a gradual shift in the mode of *seeing* nature is taking place. In the songs of the *Classic of Songs,* reflecting so much of the life of the people, plants are named specifically; the scene is the ground and brush right before one — where one dances or harvests. By the Six Dynasties, the view has moved back and become more panoramic. A case in point is the work of the poet Hsieh Ling-yün (385–433) — who has only a few rare poetic ancestors in earlier China. His aristocratic family had moved south, and he grew up in a biome that would have been considered exotic and barbarous by Confucius.

Hsieh was a mountain-lover, whose fascination with

the densely-wooded steep hills of South China (peaking between 4,000 and 6,000 feet) took him on long climbs and rambles, including one month-long trail-cutting exploration. He combined in himself the would-be Daoist recluse and the vigorous wilderness adventurer. He was also an early follower of Buddhism (a new thing at that time, limited to upper-class circles) and wrote an essay expounding "instant enlightenment."

His ambivalent pursuit of success in politics ended when he was banished to a minor position in a remote south coast town; he soon resigned totally from the administration and moved to a run-down family estate in the hills southeast of present-day Hangchow. The place and life there is detailed in his long *fu* ("rhyme-prose") called "Living in the Mountains." The farther and nearer landscapes are described quarter by quarter. The fish, birds, plants, and mammals are listed. The whole is seen as an ideal place for pursuing Daoist and Buddhist meditations. Thus,

> I cast no lines for fish.
> I spread no nets for hare.
> I have no use for barbed shafts.
> Who would set out rabbit snares or fish traps?

and he says he has "awoke to the complete propriety of loving what lives." Yet, a bit further on in the poetical essay he describes his workers, ". . . felling trees; they clear the thorns and cut bamboo," and sundry bark and reed and rush gathering activities; and charcoal-making. This faint contradiction, intensified later in history, can become a major problem: individual animals' lives are carefully spared, while the habitat that actually sustains them is heedlessly destroyed.

Hsieh is a puzzle. Arrogant and overbearing at court, he made enemies. Intensely intellectual as a Buddhist, and careless of the needs or feelings of local people, he managed to get intrigued into a charge of rebellion, and was beheaded in the marketplace. Hsieh was probably already out of place in China—he should have joined the Rock Mountain Fur Company and gone out to be a trapper. He was "wild," and as an aristocrat that took some contradictory and nasty turns. But he opened up the landscape—"mountains and waters"—to the poetic consciousness for all time, and he was a fine poet.

Mountains are always foci of spirit power in China, early perhaps as habitat for the shaman who gains "power" in the hills, a *"hsien."* Later they become a place of retreat for the Daoist practitioner of "harmonizing

with the Way" and again as sites for Buddhist monasteries. Hsieh Ling-yün plunged into the watercourses and
thickets, camped in the heights alone, walked all night
in the moonlight. These years and energies are what lies
behind what we now take to the Chinese sense of nature
as reflected in art. Hsieh is also remembered as the inven-
tor of a unique mountaineering shoe or clog—no one is
quite sure how it looked.

OXHEAD MOUNTAIN

Buddhism began and remains (at center) a set of ethi-
cal observances and meditation disciplines by means of
which hard-working human beings can win through to
self-realization and understanding the way of existence.
This effort is instructed by the content of Shakyamuni's
enlightenment experience: a realization that all things are
co-arising, mutually causing and being caused, "empty"
and without "self."

   In the time of the historical Buddha Gautama Shakyamuni, the community or Sangha of Buddhists was an
order of monks and nuns who had renounced the world. It
was held that one could not really achieve enlightenment

as a householder. Laypersons might build up a store of good merit by helping the Buddhist Order, and living virtuous lives, but the deeper experiences were not for them.

The expansion of the concept of Sangha, or Community, is a key theme in the history of Buddhism. In the Mahayana, or "Great Vehicle" branch, laymen and women are also considered worthy aspirants and almost equal practicers with monks, or, at the very least, theoretically capable of achieving enlightenment while living the householder's life. The inherent capacity to achieve enlightenment is called "Buddha-nature." At one stage in Buddhist thought (second century AD India roughly), it was held that not quite all human beings had the capacity. Those excluded, called *icchantikas,* were (to judge by description) tribal and aboriginal people who lived by hunting.

Some early Chinese Buddhist thinkers were troubled by this. In another century or so, other Indian Buddhist texts were brought to China that taught that salvation was accessible not only to all human beings but to all *sentient* beings, vindicating the Chinese thinkers. This was commonly understood to mean that animals and even plants are part of the Mahayana drama, working out their karma through countless existences, up to the point of being born into a human body. It was popularly assumed that a human body was a pre-requisite to Buddhist practice.

The eighth-century monk Chan-jan, of the T'ien T'ai sect, was one of the first to argue the final step. He concluded that non-sentient beings also have the Buddha-nature. "Therefore we may know that the single mind of a single particle of dust comprises the mind-nature of all sentient beings and Buddhas" and "The person who is of all-round perfection, knows from beginning to end that Truth is not dual and that no objects exist apart from Mind. Who then, is 'animate' and who 'inanimate'? Within the Assembly of the Lotus, all are present without division."

The Chinese philosophical appreciation of the natural world as the visible manifestation of the Dao made a happy match with Indian Mahayana eschatology. Chinese Buddhists could say, these beautiful rivers and mountains are Nirvana in the here and now. Buddhists located themselves on famous old numinous mountains, or opened up wilderness for new monasteries. In Ch'an (Zen) the masters were commonly known by the name of the mountain they lived and taught on. An early line of Ch'an, which died out in the eighth century, was called the "Oxhead

Mountain" sect. These monks did more than just admire the scenery—they were on intimate terms with the local wildlife, including tigers. The Oxhead Master Dao Lin built a nest in a tree for his meditation. Sitting up in it, he once had a conversation with the poet Po Chü-i: "Isn't it dangerous up there?" Po asked, in his Government Official's robes. "Where you are is far more dangerous" was Dao-Lin's response. In this branch of Ch'an when monks died, their bodies were left out in the forest for the animals to consume. It's also said, they had a great sense of humor.

THE CHASE IN THE PARK

In Shang dynasty times hunting had already become an upper-class sport. The old hunters' gratitude for the food received, or concern for the spirits of the dead game, had evaporated. This hunting was actually "the chase"—an expensive group activity requiring beaters who drove the game toward the waiting aristocrats who then pursued and shot with bows from chariots or horseback. Large-scale exercises of this sort were considered good training for warfare. They were followed by feasts with musicians, and slender dancers wearing diaphanous gowns. Warfare and hunting are popularly thought to be similar in spirit, and in post-civilized times this has often been the case. In hunting and gathering cultures the delicacy of preparation, and the care surrounding the act of taking life, puts hunting on a different level.

Chinese culture is strikingly free from food taboos and the upper-class cuisine is the most adventurous in the world. Even so, from Shang times on, meat was a luxury that the common people could seldom afford. Furs and feathers of animals were vastly used in the costuming of officials. Idealized instructions can be found in the *Li Chi* or "Collected Rituals" which was put together in the Han dynasty.

> When a ruler wore the robe of white fox fur, he wore one of embroidered silk over it to display it. When the guards on the right of the ruler wore tigers' fur, those on the left wore wolves' fur. An ordinary officer did not wear the fur of the white fox. Great officers wore the fur of the blue fox, with sleeves of leopard fur, and over it a jacket of dark-colored silk to display it; with fawn's fur they used cuffs of the black wild dog, with a jacket of bluish yellow silk, to display it . . .

Han dynasty ritualism has an oddly alienated quality. The nature philosophy and the plant and mineral experimentation of the Daoists, or the direct knowledge of the natural world necessary to the life of working people, is far from the highly ordered ceremoniousness that surrounded government bureaus and the court. The Han upper class did admire those who were skilled and bold in gambling for power, but it was played against a background of strict propriety. Beheading, or being boiled alive, were the fate of those who lost in the game of power.

Taking animal lives is even easier for those accustomed to taking human lives. Respect for nature comes with knowledge and contact, but attention to the observable order of nature is rarely practiced by those who think that wealth is purely a creation of human organization, labor, or ingenuity.

Still, the Emperor continued to offer sacrifices to the Earth, to Heaven, and to the great mountains and rivers of the land, all through history. Calamitous floods, or prolonged drought, would bring the State up short, and the Emperor himself would have to ask if he had somehow offended heaven. Whatever these offenses might be, it doesn't seem that destruction of wildlife habitat or waste of animal or human lives, or deforestation, was perceived as a possible offense against the un-earthly power of *T'ien,*

Sky, or Heaven. The Wealthy Governors and Emperors thus maintained large hunting parks. Edward Schafer's study of "Hunting Parks in China" (the source for all this information) suggests that they evolved from Bronze age preserves established originally to continue supplying certain wild species for the periodic state sacrifices; species whose use had been established when their numbers were far greater. By the Chou dynasty such preserves were a place for sport and recreation that might contain exotic species as well as native animals, with artificial lakes and ponds, stables, hunting lodges, and pleasure pavilions. They were an ideal place to lodge and entertain visiting heads of state. The park of the Han Emperor Wu Ti, "The Supreme Forest," was about forty by twenty miles in size and contained thirty-six detached palaces and lodges. Within its varied terrain it contained both native and exotic species of fish, birds, amphibians, and mammals. Rivers were stocked with giant softshell turtle and alligator as well as sturgeon and other fish. Caribous, sambar, rhinoceros and elephants were symbolically (and perhaps practically) located in the "south" of the preserve, and wild horses and yaks in the "north." "The ground of the Supreme Forest was prepared for the great winter hunt by the royal foresters. They burned clear a large open space and cut away brambles. Beaters, hunters and athletes readied themselves for the onslaughts of wild beasts and forest demons with spells and periapts. When the royal party arrived, the birds and beasts were driven into the cleared areas, and the slaughter began:

> A wind of feathers, a rain of blood,
> Sprinkled the countryside, covered the sky."

Parks were openly criticized by some advisors as wasteful and politically inexpedient. In Ssu-ma Hsiang-ju's *Fu* on the "Supreme Forest" the Emperor is urged to terminate the park and open it to the people for cultivation and fire-wood and fishing. It's interesting to note that no middle course is considered, such as keeping a wildlife preserve for its own natural, noumenal, or scientific interest. The virtuous alternative is to turn it over entirely to human use.

(No comparison could be made between Chinese hunting park wantonness and the destruction of animal, not to mention human, life that took place in the Roman Arena. Thousands of animals were destroyed sometimes in a few days. The constant supplying of animals to the Arena actually extincted numerous species throughout the Mediterranean basin.)

Hunting parks survived into T'ang times and later,

but new ideas from Buddhism or old ideas revived from Daoism stressing compassion for all creatures, enveloped them in a mist of moral doubt. T'ang was the high point of much poetry, and of Ch'an Buddhist creativity—but it must be remembered that it was not peopled by effete scholars in flowing robes who detested violence. It was a time of hardy Northern-derived gentry who were skilled horsepersons and archers and falconers, hard drinkers and fighters. Women were much freer then, and the custom of bound feet was yet to come. These aristocrats backed Buddhism, in part from a cosmopolitan interest in the cultural and trade exchanges possible with the little nations of Central Asia, but they kept their robust habits. An aristocratic maiden was once sought out by a suitor who was told by her parents she'd gone out hunting on horseback. That probably never happened again after T'ang.

EMPTY MOUNTAIN

China is wide. Travel was mostly on foot, maybe with a packhorse, sometimes also a riding horse. In the lowlands a network of canals provided channels for slow-moving passenger boats as well as the freight barges. Travellers moved by boat on the big rivers — slowly and laboriously upstream, pulled by men on shore, and swiftly and boisterously back down. Boats sailed across the lakes and slow-moving lower river reaches. Horse and ox carts moved men and materials in the alluvial plains and rolling hills. In the mountains and deserts, long caravans of pack animals moved the goods of empire.

Government officials were accustomed to travelling weeks or even months to a new appointment, with their whole family. Buddhist monks and Daoist wanderers had a tradition of freely walking for months or years on end. In times of turmoil whole populations of provinces, and contending armies, might be tangled in frenzied travel on the paths and waterways. It was said, "If a man has his heart set on great things 10,000 *li* are like his front yard." So the people of the watersheds of the Yang and Huang Rivers came to know the shape of their territory.

The officials and monks (and most poets were one or the other) were an especially mobile group of literate people. Travellers' prose or rhymed-prose descriptions of landscapes were ingenious in evoking the complexity of gorges and mountains. Regional geographies with detailed accounts of local biomes were encouraged. Hsieh Ling-yun's *fu* on his mountain place is descriptive and didactic—but his poems in the *shih* (lyric) form already manifest the quiet intensity that becomes the definitive quality of Chinese *shih* poetry in its greatest creative T'ang and Sung dynasty phases.

The Chinese and Japanese traditions carry within them the most sensitive, mind-deepening poetry of the natural world ever written by civilized people. Because these poets were men and women who dealt with budgets, taxes, penal systems, and the overthrow of governments, they had a heart-wrenching grasp of the contradictions that confront those who love the natural world and are yet tied to the civilized. This must be one reason why Chinese poetry is so widely appreciated by contemporary Occidentals.

Yet it's hard to pin down what a "Chinese nature poem" might be, and why so effective. They are not really about landscapes or scenery. Space of distant hills becomes space in life; a condition the poet-critic Lu Chi called "calm transparency." Mountains and rivers were seen to be the visible expression of cosmic principles; the cosmic principles go back into silence, non-being, emptiness; a Nothing that can produce the ten thousand things, and the ten thousand things will have that marvelous emptiness still at the center. So the poems are also "silent."

Much is left unsaid, and the reverberation or mirroring — a flight of birds across the mind of the sky — leaves an alterimage to be savoured, and finally leaves no trace. The Chinese poetic tradition is also where human emotions are revealed; where an official can be vulnerable and frail. Lu Chi says poetry starts with a lament for fleeting life, and regard for the myriad growing things — taking thought of the great virtuous deeds of people past, and the necessity of making "maps" for the future. Chinese poetry steps out of narrow human-centered affairs into a big-spirited world of long time, long views, and natural processes; and comes back to a brief moment in a small house by a fence.

The strain of nostalgia for the self-contained hard-working but satisfying life of the farmer goes along somehow with delight in jumbled gorges. Nature is finally not a "wilderness" but a habitat, the best of habitats, a place where you not only practice meditation or strive for a vision, but grow vegetables, play games with the children, and drink wine with friends. In this there is a politics of a special order — the Chinese nature poet is harking back to the Neolithic village, never forgotten and constantly returned to mind by the Daoist classics — as a model for a better way of life. Sectarian Daoism and its secret societies fermented a number of armed peasant uprisings through history that unwittingly had "neolithic" on their standards. "Playing with your grandchildren"—"growing chrysanthemums"—"watching the white clouds"—are phrases from a dream of pre-feudal or post-revolutionary society.

Chinese poets of these centuries were not biologists or primitive hunters, though, and their poetics did not lead them to certain precisions. What they found were landscapes to match inner moods—and a deep sense of reverence for this obvious actual mystery of a real world. In Burton Watson's analysis of nature imagery in T'ang poems he finds more references to non-living phenomena than living, and over half of those looking upward to sky, weather, wind, clouds, and moon. Downward: rivers, waters and mountains predominate. Among living things willow and pine are the most-mentioned trees, but the specific names of herbaceous plants and flowers are few—with "flowers" usually meaning the blossoms of trees like cherry or peach. Wild goose is the most common bird, associated with being separated from a friend; and monkey the most common mammal—because of its mournful cry. Cicada and moth are the most common insect. The point is made that many natural references are used for their symbolic or customary human associations, and not for intrinsic natural qualities. No doubt the oral poetry of a pre-literate people will have more acquaintance with the actual living creatures as numinous intelligences in furry or scaly bodies. But this does not detract from what the Chinese poems are, highly disciplined and formal poems that open us to the dilemma of having "regard for the myriad growing things" while being literate monks or administrators or wives of officials in the world's first "great society." The reign of the Emperor Hsuan Tsung (712–756) is considered one of the high points of Chinese cultural history: the poets Wang Wei, Li Po, and Tu Fu were at the height of their powers during those years, and so were the brilliant and influential Ch'an Masters Shen-hui, Nan-yüeh, Ma-tsu, and Po-chang. The national population may have been as high as 60 million.

I first came onto Chinese poems in translation at nineteen, when my ideal of nature was a 45 degree ice slope on a volcano, or an absolutely virgin rain forest. They helped me to "see" fields, farms, tangles of brush, the azaleas in the back of an old brick apartment. They freed me from excessive attachment to wild mountains, with their almost subliminal way of presenting even the wildest hills as a place where people, also, live.

Empty mountains:
>no one to be seen,

Yet—hear—
>human sounds and echoes.

>Returning sunlight

>enters the dark woods;

Again shining
>on green moss, above.

WANG WEI

Ink and Charcoal

One of the earliest descriptions of the vegetation of China is by Li Tao-yuan, fifth century AD. He travelled the whole region from Vietnam to the far deserts of Sinkiang:

> . . . In the Hwang-Ho valley, he noted thickets of *Corylus* and other shrubs; pasture; plains covered with miles of *Ephedra;* forests of elms; pines; *Juniperus* growing on cliffs and on the peaks of distant mountains; and mixed hardwood forests.
>
> Farther south, in the upper Yangtze Valley, he noted bamboo thickets; *Cupressus* on rocky cliffs; and in the gorges, tall forests with numerous monkeys. In the lower Yangtze Valley he found oak forests, evergreen forests . . . in northern Viet-nam he found dense forests and immense swamps that swarmed with herds of elephants and rhinoceros.*

*C.W. Wang. *The Forests of China*, Marla Moors Cabot Foundation Publications Series #5 (Cambridge: Harvard University Press, 1961) p. 19

Early T'ang dynasty China (618–906 AD) with its 50 million people had a very energetic economy. The balance was already clearly shifting away from a "world of human beings winning a living from a vast wild landscape," to a condition of wild habitats shrinking before a relentlessly expanding agricultural society.

The grounds of temples became the last refuges of huge old trees; in fact the present-day reconstruction of original forest cover in north China is done to a great extent by plotting the distribution of relict stands on temple grounds. In the higher elevations and in the remoter regions some forest remains to this day, but other than temples, the grounds of the tombs of emperors and royal hunting preserves were about the only areas firmly set aside and protected. The importance of watershed protection was understood and sometimes enforced by policy; the emperor Hsüan Tsung forbade wood cutting on Mount Lim, near the capital. But the forests were slowly nibbled away, without any national forest policy ever coming into being. The history of environment in China can be understood in terms of the frog in hot water. A frog tossed into a pan of boiling water, it is said, will jump right out. A frog placed in a pan of cold water over a slow flame will not leap out, and soon it's too late.

That tool of the poet and painter, the inkstick (even more essential to the Chinese administration), was responsible for much deforestation.

> The best source of black ink for the clerks and scholars of the nation was soot, made by burning pine. Even before T'ang times, the ancient pines of the mountains of Shantung had been reduced to carbon, and now the busy brushes of the vast T'ang bureaucracy were rapidly bringing baldness to the T'ai-hang mountains between Shansi and Hopei.*

The original climax forest of China south of the Huai River was an evergreen broadleaf forest. These were trees of the laurel family such as cinnamon and sassafras, plus chinquapins and liquidambers. Most of the wooded landscape to be seen in south China today is secondary growth. Pines and brush replace deciduous hardwoods after logging or fire. Writing of the lower Yangtze, C.W. Wang notes:

*Edward Schafer. "The Conservation of Nature Under the T'ang Dynasty," *Journal of the Economic and Social History of the Orient* 5. (1962) p. 300

The lower elevations, especially the alluvial plains, have long been under cultivation, and the natural vegetation has been altered almost beyond recognition. The existing vegetation outside of cultivated areas consists mostly of pine and hardwood mixed stands, *Pinus massoniana* and *Cunninghamia* plantations and scrubby vegetation.*

The great plain that reaches from the lower Yangtze River north almost to Manchuria has no original plant life left except salt-adapted plants on the coast. It was once a dense forest abundant with beeches, maples, catalpa, chestnut, walnut, elm, and ash.

Planted farm woodlots are common, however:

Contrary to general belief, the Plain, except for the large cities, is not only self-sufficient in its wood supply, but it produces poplar logs for match factories, and exports Paulownia wood to Japan.†

The forests of northeast Manchuria are, or were, the last large-scale virgin timberlands in China. In 1913 Arthur Sowerby wrote:

*Wang, p. 103   † Wang, p. 85

But the forest! Time and again it riveted one's attention as its millions and millions of trees appeared, clothing the hills, ridges upon ridges, to the horizon. There was no break in the sea of green; there was no gap visible.*

It is thought that tigers were originally a northern animal, and that some of them moved south, ultimately as far as what is now Bali. The Siberian tiger, with its whiter stripes and longer fur, is the largest. It was considered the Master of the Wild by many Siberian tribal people. There are stories of mountain shaman types, "immortals" and priests who were on friendly terms with tigers. Shih K'o's whimsical tenth-century painting shows a Ch'an monk napping over the back of a tiger that is also asleep.

Ranging from the subarctic to the tropics, the fauna of China was varied and rich. An east-west line can be drawn following the Tsin-ling mountains and the Huai River that serves as a rough boundary between northern-Asian animals and the animals that range up from the south. The Siberian roe deer comes as far south as these mountains as do the yak, wild horse, and wapiti.

*Wang, p. 35.

Elephants were widespread in China in early civilized times, and wandered from the south as far north as the plains of the Yellow River. Macaque monkeys are now pretty much in the south, but must have ranged north because they are still found wild in Japan in all the islands except Hokkaido. The Indian Muntjac never goes north of central Yunnan. Cats, lynxes, wolves, martens, bears, weasels, wild pigs, antelopes, sika deer, goral, serow, goats, and many other small mammals mingle through both zones. Bird life can be broken into regions too, but there is obviously more mingling than with mammals. Ducks which winter in India or Vietnam may be summering in Siberia.

One guide to environmental practice in China was a kind of farmers' annual schedule, called the *Yüeh Ling* ("Monthly Ordinances"). In describing the timing of appropriate tasks and preparations through the cycle of the year, it takes a conservationist tone, with "warning against gathering eggs, destroying nests, and hunting young or pregnant animals." * It allows an autumn hunting season. The teachings of Buddhism were never accepted by the Chinese to the point that total prohibi-

---

*Schafer 1962, p. 289

tion of taking life could be made law, although Emperor Hstian Tsung actually tried. At one time he even issued an edict banning the killing of dogs and chickens:

> Dogs, as guardians and defenders, and chickens, which watch for daybreak, have utility for mankind comparable to that of other domestic animals. We may rightly make the virtue of loving life extend everywhere, and, from now on, the slaughter and killing of these will in no case be allowed.*

Such an edict was unenforceable. So with the shrinking forests, animal and bird life also declined. The pressure on certain species was intensified by their real or supposed use for medicine. All parts of the tiger were considered of medical value. The horn of the rhinoceros was prized as material for a beautiful wine cup, and the powdered horn greatly valued as an antidote to poison. So the rhinoceros is no longer found in China, and illegal poaching today on rhinoceros preserves in India is for the Chinese market. Wild elephants "trampled the cultivated fields of Honan and Hupeh in the fifth Christian

*Schafer 1962, p. 303

century"* and the tribal *Man* people of the south domesticated them, training them even to perform at parties for
Chinese envoys. Elephants also are gone now. A more
widespread animal, the Sika deer, has almost been exter-
minated for the trade in antlers-in-velvet, also of value as
medicine. "Economic interest also prevented the protection of kingfishers, whose feathers were used in jewelry,
of muskdeer, which provided a popular scent for ladies
of fashion, of martens, whose furs gave style to martial
hats, and of alligators, whose tough hides were used to
cover drums."†

Dr. Edward Schafer's paper on "The Conservation of
Nature under the T'ang Dynasty" sums it up:

> All of the psychological conditions necessary to pro-
> duce sound policy for the protection of nature, both
> as an economic and esthetic resource, were present in
> T'ang times. But though enlightened monarchs issued
> edicts, conformable to the best morality of their times,
> these were ignored by their successors. In short, there

---

*Edward H. Schafer. *The Vermilion Bird: T'ang Images of the South*
(Berkeley: UC Press, 1967) p. 224
†Schafer 1962, pp. 301–2

was no permanent embodiment of these advanced ideas in constitutional forms. And so they were ultimately ineffective.*

Moreover, the common sense of farmers embodied in the *Yüeh Ling* (of which Schafer says, "It appears that the *Yüeh Ling* was a more important source of moral conservatism in that period than the doctrines of either the Buddhists or the Daoists"[†]) was often directly contradicted by the official class:

Sometimes even city parks and avenues suffered because of the demand for fuel. For example, certain officials in the capital city devised a scheme to finance donatives for the imperial troops, at a time when firewood was dear and silk was cheap, by cutting down the trees which embellished the city, and exchanging the wood for textiles at great profit.[††]

* Schafer 1962, p. 308
[†] Schafer 1962, p. 289
[††] Schafer 1962, p. 299

The environmental good sense of the people was not unrelated to their ongoing folk religion and the power of countryside shamanesses. Just as wild habitat was being steadily cut back, the ancient local shrines of the people were being gradually demolished by Confucian officials:

> A notable example is that of Ti Jen-chieh — in our own century transformed in the sagacious Judge Dee of van Gulik's detective novels — who after an inspection tour immediately south of the Yangtze in the seventh century, was gratified to report that he had destroyed seventeen hundred unauthorized shrines in that region.*

And in the eleventh century, the brilliant scientist-humanist-official Shen Kua experimented with making ink out of naturally-occurring petroleum, called "stone oil," saying:

> The black color was as bright as lacquer and could not be matched by pinewood resin ink ... I think this invention of mine will be widely adopted. The petroleum

---

*Edward H. Schafer. *The Divine Woman: Dragon Ladies and Rain Maidens in T'ang Literature* (Berkeley: UC Press, 1973) pp. 10–11

is abundant and more will be formed in the earth while supplies of pine-wood may be exhausted. Pine forests in Ch'i and Lu have already become sparse. This is now happening in the Tai Hang mountains. All the woods south of the Yangtze and west of the capital are going to disappear in time if this goes on, yet the ink-makers do not yet know the benefit of petroleum smoke.*

He was one thousand years ahead of his time.

*Sir Joseph Needham. *Science and Civilization in China*, Vol. III (Cambridge, UK: Cambridge University Press, 1959) p. 609

Walls Within Walls

High population, deforestation, a cash economy, and tribal nomad horsemen bring a partial end to one of the peak urban cultures: Sung Dynasty China.

CITY WALLS

Dwelling within walls-within-walls was normal for the Chinese people of the plains and valleys. In the Former-Han dynasty there were an estimated 37,844 walled settlements of various sizes, with perhaps 60 million people living behind them.* Walls are a striking part of the Chinese landscape even today, the gently slanted stone walls of a provincial capital, broken by occasional towers that project two or three stories higher yet, rising through the mist fronting a river or lake, or mirrored in half-flooded fields.

The early Neolithic settlements of the Yang-shao type had no walls. Instead they were surrounded by ditches or moats about 15 feet wide and deep. These were probably

---

* Yi-fu Tuan. *China* (Chicago: Aldine, 1970).

to keep out animals; deer are notorious nibblers on orchards and vegetable gardens. Digs of Yang-shao settlements have turned up few, if any, fighting weapons. Lung-shan type settlements of the later Neolithic have tamped-earth fortifications and weapons.*

Around the fifth century BC, as the Eastern Chou dynasty slipped toward the era of "Warring States," the basic style of walled city began to take shape.

> The type consisted of at least three contrasting spatial units: a small enclosure which was the aristocratic and administrative centre, mixed (in early times) with dependent tradesmen and artisans; industrial and commercial quarters, with residences, in a large enclosure; farmlands immediately beyond the city walls. In the warring states period sometimes three successive ramparts were built, suggesting a need to extend protection to increasingly large areas of commercial activity. Another change lay in the strengthening of the outer walls at the expense of the walls of the inner citadel, which were allowed to go into decay.[†]

* Kwang-chih Chang. *The Archeology of Ancient China* (New Haven: Yale University Press, 1977) p. 152
[†] Tuan, p. 67

The city of Hsia-tu, in the state of Yen, is estimated to have been ten square miles within the walls. There were also the "great walls" to keep out the northern nomad tribesmen, the walls originally built by the states of Ch'in, Yen, and Chao. When Ch'in became the first all-China empire, 221 BC, it joined together previous sections to make a more continuous barrier.

The dominant element of the Han dynasty townscape was the wall. It separated a settlement from the outlying fields, and by creating an enclosure facilitated the regimentation of life within . . . it had the character of a succession of walled-in rectangles. There was the town wall with gates on the four sides. Within the wall the settlement was partitioned into a number of wards. Ch'ang-an itself had as many as 160 wards. Streets separated the wards, which were in turn surrounded by walls. Each ward had only one gate opening to the street during Han times and contained up to one hundred households, each of which was again surrounded by a wall. The inhabitants, to get out of town, would thus have to pass through three sets of gates: that of their house, that of their ward, and that of their town. Moreover, all the gates were guarded and closed up at night.*

* Tuan, p. 104

Climbing over these walls after dark is a staple in Chinese storytelling: lovers, criminals, and spies.

T'ang dynasty cities had a little more night life than those of the Han, and larger, looser markets, with special quarters for the Persian, Turkish, and Arab traders. The plan of the capital city of Ch'ang-an followed in good part the old ritual idcal — "The Polar star and the celestial meridian writ small became the royal palace and the main north-south streets through the city." * The north-south streets were 450 feet wide. The upper classes were in the eastern sector and the working people in the west. Each wing had its own market area. There were also vacant lots with vegetable gardens and pasture within the walls. The great city was spacious and open.

Such city planning seemed to work, but no one could have foreseen the relentless (if fluctuating) rise of population, especially after the year 1100, when the national number first exceeded 100 million. Part of the later rise reflects an increase in the size of the Chinese territory and the inclusion of people considered non-Chinese in earlier times. After 1100 there were five urban centers with over a million people each south of the Huai River.

* Tuan, p. 106

Flying Money

Between the ninth and the thirteenth centuries China became what it basically was to be into modern times. During the three centuries of the Sung dynasty not only people but wealth and high culture moved south and in towards towns. In the early twelfth century only six percent of the population was urban, but by the fourteenth an estimated 33 percent were living in or around large cities.*

In the second phase of the T'ang dynasty, after An Lu-shan's rebellion, the tax base was changed from per capita to a straight land tax. This meant that wealthy manors which had long been exempt began to pay taxes. It was the first of a series of shifts or tendencies with profound effects. Some of the changes were:

- from a people's corvée army to an army of mercenaries
- manor-owning country gentlemen often became absentee landlords

* Mark Elvin. *The Pattern of the Chinese Past* (Stanford: Stanford University Press, 1973) p. 175

- cumbersome metal coin was replaced by paper money
- from a rustic naïveté to a street-wise hedonism
- from an interest in cultural diversity to a China-centered cultural chauvinism
- from regional agricultural self-sufficiency to cash-crop specialization
- from status determined by family connections to a greater emphasis on status derived from high ranks in government examinations
- from hiking through the mountains to tending an artificially wild-looking backyard garden

The society that began to emerge we can recognize at many points as analogous to what we now consider "modern"—but more convivial and peaceful. It was the best society one could hope to see in a world of high population and dwindling resources. It was a kind of human cultural climax, from which the contemporary world may still have much to learn. The sophistication of social devices was remarkable:

Local tax collectors developed the corollary function of wholesalers or brokers, gathering the local surplus of agricultural or manufactured goods for sale to transport merchants. The latter ranged from itinerant peddlers to large-scale, monopolistic operators. An extensive network of inns that developed to accommodate these traveling merchants became the inn system that was to continue with little change until recent times.*

Old and already effective farming skills were enhanced by new tools, seeds, plants, and a broad exchange of information via the exhaustive agricultural encyclopaedias and treatises now made available by mass woodblock printing. The poet and administrator Su Shih wrote a prose piece on a unique new rice-transplanting device that looked like a wooden hobbyhorse. In rice seed alone a revolution took place: a drought-resistant seed from central Vietnam came to be used widely. It could be grown on poorer soil, and so expanded available rice acreage. "By Sung times almost all of the types in use before the middle of Tang had disappeared . . . a southern Sung gazetteer for the county of Ch'ang-shu in the lower Yangtze delta lists twenty-one kinds of moderate

* Edwin O. Reischauer and John K. Fairbank. *East Asia: The Great Tradition* (New York: Houghton Mifflin, 1960) p. 213

gluten rice, eight of high gluten rice, four of low gluten rice and ten miscellaneous varieties as being cultivated there."* Mark Elvin says that by the thirteenth century China had the most sophisticated agriculture in the world, with India the only possible rival.†

Increased contact with the market made the Chinese peasantry into a class of adaptable, rational, profit-oriented, petty entrepreneurs. A wide range of new occupations opened up in the countryside. In the hills, timber was grown for the booming boatbuilding industry and for the construction of houses in the expanding cities. Vegetables and fruit were produced for urban consumption. All sorts of oils were pressed for cooking, lighting, waterproofing, and to go into haircreams and medicines. Sugar was refined, crystallized, used as a preservative.

Fish were raised in ponds and reservoirs to the point where the rearing of newly-hatched young fish for stock became a major business.††

*Elvin, p. 121
† Elvin, p. 129
†† Elvin, p. 167

Trade and commerce weren't new to China, though. In the first century BC Ssu-ma Ch'ien wrote:

> . . . from the age of Emperor Shun and the Hsia dynasty down to the present, ears and eyes have always longed for the ultimate in beautiful sounds and forms, mouths have desired to taste the best in grass-fed and grain-fed animals, bodies have delighted in ease and comfort, and hearts have swelled with pride at the glories of powers and ability. So long have these habits been allowed to permeate the lives of the people that, though one were to go from door to door preaching the subtle arguments of the Daoists, he could never succeed in changing them.*

Ssu-ma did short biographies of famous commoners who made fortunes by buying low and selling high, gambling on surplus and dearth. The merchant Chi-jan of the fifth century BC said, "When an article has become extremely expensive, it will surely fall in price, and when it has become extremely cheap then the price will begin to rise.

---

*Ssu-ma Ch'ien, translated by Burton Watson. *Records of the Grand Historian*, Vol. II (New York: Columbia University Press, 1961) pp. 476–7

Dispose of expensive goods as though they were so much filth and dirt; buy up cheap goods as though they were pearls and jade. Wealth and currency should be allowed to flow as freely as water!"*

This trade was conducted with rolls of silk, bales of rice, salt, or copper cash as the media of exchange. Cash was often scarce, and by mid-Tang it was noted that mining the copper and minting and transporting new coin cost twice as much as its face value as money. All sorts of "flying money"—promissory notes, letters of credit, and private-issue proto-money—were succeeded by government-issue paper money in the eleventh century. During the thirteenth century, and under the Mongols in the early fourteenth, the government even accepted paper money for the payment of taxes! Marco Polo was astonished to see paper used just as though it were metal. If the flow of currency began to falter, the government instantly offered silver or gold as payment for paper. "For 17 or 18 years the value of paper money did not fluctuate." †

*Ssu-ma, p. 48
† Elvin, p. 160

THE SOUTHERN CAPITAL

In the coastal province of Chekiang, south of Shanghai, there are still some upland areas of Miao population. In the fifth century AD, when Hsieh Ling-yun walked the hills and worked on his rural estate, the greater part of the province was considered barbarian. It is named for the Che River, which reaches into the southern slopes of the Huang mountains, and the 3,000-foot hills on the Kiangsi-Anhwei border. The river is famous for the tidal bore that plays in its mouth at Hangchou bay. A decade after the fall of the Northern Sung capital K'ai-feng to the Juchen (Chin), the town of Lin-an, at the rivermouth, was declared the new capital. The emigre emperor, his court, and crowds of refugees of the northern ruling class settled in. The name was changed to Hang-chou.

In earlier times the Lin-an area had been a marsh. The main river was channelized and subsidiary streams dammed in the fifth century AD. The original town grew then on land between the lake thus formed, "West Lake," and the main Che River. It has come to be considered one of the most scenic places in China. Great care has been taken to keep the shallow lake clean. It was a true public park, with laws against planting water-chestnut (which would rapidly spread) or dumping trash in the water. Public pavilions, docks, and shade areas were built. Zoning restrictions designated acceptable architectural styles. Buddhist temples were looked on with favor; one of the most famous structures overlooking the lake was the pagoda at Thunder Point. Built of blue glazed brick, it was 170 feet high.

Po Chu-i had served as prefect here in the ninth century, and Su Shih did major maintenance and improvement on the lake when he was briefly prefect in the late eleventh century. The causeway on the lake is named after him.*

In 1136 Hang-chou had a population of around 200,000. In 1170 this had become half a million, and in 1275 it was well over a million and perhaps the largest single concentration of human beings in the world at that time.† It may also have been the richest. The capital fell to the Mongols in 1279, after a siege of several years. Marco Polo was in the city soon after it surrendered (he worked for Kublai Khan for 17 years) and has left eloquent description:

---

*Jacques Gernet. *Daily Life in China on the Eve of the Mongol Invasion* (Stanford: Stanford University Press, 1962) p. 51–52
† Gernet, p. 28

On one side is a lake of fresh water, very clear. On the other is a huge river, which entering by many channels, diffused throughout the city, carries away all its filth and then flows into the lake, from which it flows out towards the Ocean. This makes the air very wholesome. And through every part of the city it is possible to travel either by land or by these streams. The streets and watercourses alike are very wide, so that carts and boats can readily pass along them to carry provisions for the inhabitants.

There are ten principal marketplaces, not to speak of innumerable local ones. These are square, being a half a mile each way. In front of them lies a main thoroughfare, 40 paces wide, which runs straight from one end of the city to the other. It is crossed by many bridges . . . and every four miles, there is one of these squares. . . . And in each of these squares, three days in the week, there is a gathering of 40 to 50 thousand people, who come to market bringing everything that could be desired to sustain life. There is always abundance of victuals, both wild game, such as roebuck, stags, harts, hares, and rabbits, and of fowls, such as partridges, pheasants, francolins, quails, hens, capons, and as many ducks and geese as can be told. . . . Then there are the shambles, where they slaughter the bigger animals, such as calves, oxen, kid, and lambs, whose flesh is eaten by the rich and upper classes. The others, the lower orders, do not scruple to eat all sorts of unclean flesh.

All the ten squares are surrounded by high buildings, and below these are shops in which every sort of craft is practiced and every sort of luxury is on sale, including spices, gems, and pearls. In some shops nothing is sold but spiced rice wine, which is being made all the time, fresh and very cheap.*

Hang-chou was kept spotless. The authorities had the streets cleaned and refuse piled at key points where it was loaded into boats. The boats in turn converged and took it out to the country in convoys. Nightsoil (human waste) was collected by corporations each with their own gathering territory who sold it to the intensive truck gardens of the eastern suburbs.† (Contrary to common opinion in the West, the use of nightsoil does not pose a health problem if it is aged properly before applying—as it usually is. I

---

*Marco Polo. *The Travels*, translated by R.E. Latham (New York: Penguin, 1958) p. 187

†Gernet, p. 43

poured and gardened with it myself as a Zen student in Japan.) Marco Polo's account of what he and the Mongols called *Kinsai* (from *Hsing-ts'ai,* "temporary residence of the emperor") describes 3,000 public baths. "I assure you they are the finest baths and the best and biggest in the world—indeed they are big enough to accommodate a hundred men or women at once." *

The rich, bustling life of thirteenth-century southern China set the tone for seventeenth- and eighteenth-century Osaka and Tokyo. (In reading Jacques Gernet and Marco Polo on Hang-chou, I find myself reliving moments in the Kyoto of the 1950s and '60s. A coffee shop on Kawaramachi full of chic western-dressed youth, called "Den-en" after T'ao Ch'ien's poetry of "fields and gardens." A public bath in the Gion proud of its tradition of extra-hot bathwater, to please the ladies of the quarter and the late-night drinkers and gamblers. A small modern-style bar called Tesu—where when asked what the name meant, the modish lady who owned it said, "Why of course, from *Tess of the D'Urbervilles.*") Such cities, though crowded, are not dangerous. Our American image of a city as a faceless network of commercial canyons, bordered by suburbs where no one ever goes on foot,

* Polo, p. 143

reflects little of the conditions of city life in pre-modern cultures. Like a huge village, Hang-chou had about 15 major festivals a year. In one of these the emperor opened up part of the palace grounds for the street entertainers to put on a street-life show for the people of the court.

Marco Polo:

> The natives of Kinsia are men of peace . . . they have no skills in handling arms and do not keep any in their houses. There is prevalent among them a dislike and distaste for strife or any sort of disagreement. They pursue their trades and handicrafts with great diligence and honesty. They love one another so devotedly that a whole district might seem, from the friendly and neighborly spirit that rules among men and women, to be a single household.

> If they come across some poor man by day, who is unable to work on account of illness, they have him taken to one of the hospitals, of which there are great numbers throughout the city, built by the ancient kings and lavishly endowed. And when he is cured, he is compelled to practice some trade.*

* Polo, pp. 191–2

Life in the city went on virtually without cease; the bars and brothels closed around two A.M. and the *abattoirs* started up at three. Till late at night, illuminated pleasure boats drifted on the lake with clan or guild or fraternity parties singing and drinking and eating. Boats of all sizes and styles were available for hire.

> They are roofed over with decks on which stand men with poles which they thrust into the bottom of the lake. . . . The deck is painted inside with various colours and designs and so is the whole barge, and all around it are windows that can be opened or shut so that the banqueters ranged along the sides can look this way and that and feast their eyes on the diversity and beauty of the scenes through which they are passing. . . . On one side it skirts the city, so that the barge commands a distant view of all its grandeur and loveliness, its temples, palaces, monasteries, and gardens with their towering trees, running down to the water's edge. On the lake itself is the endless procession of barges thronged with pleasure-seekers. For the people of this city think of nothing else, once they have done the work of their craft or their trade, but to spend a part of the day with their womenfolk or with

hired women in enjoying themselves whether in these barges or in riding about the city in carriages.*

Produce and firewood came into the city by boat, the latter some distance from the hills of the interior. At the very least 70 tons of rice a day were consumed. Shoppers at the market discriminated between "new-milled rice, husked winter rice, first quality white rice, rice with lotus-pink grains, yellow-eared rice, rice on the stalk, ordinary rice, glutinous rice"[†] and many others. There were some great places to eat:

> Formerly . . . the best-known specialties were the sweet soya soup at the Mixed-wares Market, pig cooked in ashes in front of Longevity-and-Compassion Palace, the fish-soup of Mother Sung outside the Cash-reserve Gate, and rice served with mutton. Later, around the years 1241-1252, there were, among other things, the boiled pork from Wei-the-Big-Knife at the Cat Bridge, and the honey fritters from Chou-number-five in front of the Five-span Pavilion.[††]

* Polo, p. 190
[†] Gernet, p. 86
[††] Gernet, p. 137

By the tenth century, woodblock printing was in common use. Literacy and learning spread, so that the earlier, simpler division of society into an illiterate mass and a literate Confucian elite no longer applied. Merchants, wandering monks, peasant-entrepreneurs, daughters of substantial merchants — all read books. "Catalogs, encyclopedias, and treatises appeared which dealt with a wide variety of topics: monographs on curious rocks, on jades, on coins, on inks, on bamboos, on plum-trees . . . treatises on painting and calligraphy; geographical works. The first general and unofficial histories of China made their appearance." * The West Lake, already famous from its association with two of China's most highly regarded poets, gave its name to the "Poetry Society of the Western Lake" which counted both natives of the city and visiting literati among its members. It held picnics, banquets, and competitions, and the winning poems were circulated through the society. Hang-chou was a world of soft-handed scholars, dainty-stepping maidens raised behind closed doors, hustling town dandies, urban laborers, just-arrived country girls whose looks would determine if they'd work in a back kitchen or a teahouse.

* Gernet, pp. 229–30

The best rhinoceros skins are to be found at Ch'ien's,
     as you go down from the canal to the little Ch'ing-
     hu lake.
The finest turbans at K'ang-number-three's in the
     street of the Worn Cash-coin;
The best place for used books at the bookstalls
     under the big trees near the summer-house of the
     Orange Tree Garden;
Wicker cages in Ironwire Lane,
Ivory combs at Fei's
Folding fans at Coal Bridge.*

Most people rose early, finished work early, and left time in the afternoon for shopping and social calls. About three A.M. in the summer, and four in the winter, the bells of the Buddhist temples on the outskirts would begin to boom. At four or five in the morning, Buddhist and Daoist monks were walking down the lanes, beating a rhythm on the hand-held "wooden fish" and calling out the morning's weather—"a light snow just starting"—and announcing the day's events, whether preparations for a festival, a court reception, or a building-code hearing.

*Gernet, p. 85

"Imperial audiences were held at five or six o'clock in the morning. Seven o'clock was considered to be already late in the day." *

Hats and Buckles

At the time of the Mongol conquest poor people still had some meat to eat, a little pork or fish. In recent centuries meat has been a once- or twice-a-year treat. The wealthy could also afford wild game. There were no sanctions, apparently, against market hunting, though shoppers were warned to beware of donkey or horsemeat being sold as venison.† The deforestation that had been predicted by Shen Kua two centuries earlier (he was almost exactly contemporary with Su Shih) was well underway. Sung economic expansion stimulated remarkable industrial development—"comparable to that which took place during the earlier phases of England's industrial revolution." The quantity of iron produced during the Northern Sung period was not matched again until the nineteenth century. Tuan Yi-fu summarizes:

*Gernet, p. 182   † Gernet, p. 137

The rapid growth of ironworks exerted pressure on timber resources, which were already heavily pressed to meet the needs of large city populations and of shipbuilding. Many hundreds of thousands of tons of charcoal were swallowed up by the metal industries. In addition, there was the demand for charcoal in the manufacture of salt, alum, bricks, tiles and liquor. The Northern Sung period must be seen as a time of rapid deforestation. North China suffered first. . . . Firewood and charcoal for the cities and the industries had to be transported from the South. There was an acute shortage which was partially met by the effective substitution of coal for charcoal in the eleventh century.*

Wetlands were drained. It seems the expansion of rice-fields into "wastelands" or marshes often went against the interests and desires of the local people, who relied on ponds and estuaries for fishing and gathering edible water plants. Large landowners or the government itself undertook these projects, looking for profits or taxes. (The chain of events that led to the execution of Hsieh

*Tuan, pp. 130–1

Ling-yun started with his plan to drain the Hui-chung lake, near the modern town of Shao-hsing. This lake was on public land, but a landowner of Hsieh's stature could usually have expected to get away with it. The governor of the province, however, was an old rival, and his enmity combined with the reports of clashes between local peasants and Hsieh's armed retainers opened the way to a charge of rebellion.) In the late Sung the government encouraged small farmers, by granting tax exemptions, to go into marshy grounds on the Yangtze delta. The loss was not only wild food previously gathered by the poor, but habitat for water-fowl and other members of the marshy ecosystems.

Along with wetlands and forests, the people as a whole were losing accurate knowledge of nature. For the last few centuries it has been believed in China that tortoises were female to the male of snakes; a bronze statuette shows a tortoise and snake copulating. The correct information of sunburned naked boys or old fishermen who knew better became no account. The harmless gecko (wall lizard) and the toad came to be considered poisonous. The big-shouldered wild boar, *Sus scrofa,* which appears in Han hunting scenes, and is still the type of pig in T'ang art, is replaced in the art of later dynasties by the sway-backed droop-eared domestic pig type.*

From Shang to Ch'in times animals and insects appear in Chinese art in the conventionalized forms sometimes associated with the "Scythian" art of ancient central Asia. None of the designs are floral, and those which seem so are actually loops and spirals of insects and reptiles.† Realistic animals appear from the Han dynasty onward—deer being chased by hounds, a tiger with a collar. Later representation of animals tends more and more to cleave to symbolic and legendary significance. "Everything in their painting, carved panels, lacquered screens, pieces of tapestry or embroidery, stone bas-reliefs, or the decorations on furniture and buildings means something. It is this fact that helps to explain why certain animals appear with great frequency, while others equally well known occur but seldom, or are altogether absent."††

Thus leopards were far more common in China than tigers, yet are rarely seen in art. Other animals that seldom appear are the hedgehog, shrews and moles, the common

---

* Arthur de Carle Sowerby. *Nature in Chinese Art* (New York: John Day, 1940) pp. 65, 99
† Sowerby, p. 129
†† Sowerby, p. 44

muskshrew of the southeast, the scaly anteater, the civets, and many rodents including the porcupine. Insects are often represented in many media. In Han times carved jade cicada were placed in the mouth of the dead. Entirely lifelike hairy-clawed crabs were constructed in bronze. In Sowerby's study on "nature in Chinese art" we find included a glass snuff bottle with a butterfly in low relief on black glass; an unidentified fish in jade; a marble seal with a toad carved on the top; realistic scroll paintings of carp, minnows, knife-fish, mandarin fish, catfish, and bitterlings; a split bamboo with a wasp inside all carved in ivory; an unglazed statue of a Bactrian camel; a lifelike elephant with a harness from the Six Dynasties period; and a bronze buckle inlaid in silver, in the form of a rhinoceros.

The poor rhinoceros. A hat of some sort, and a girdle or belt with a buckle, were essential to male dress. Gernet says:

These were the two things which distinguished the Chinese from the barbarian . . . the finest girdles had plaques or buckles in jade, in gold, or in rhinoceros horn. The horn was imported from India, and in particular Bengal, which was supposed to have the best horn. . . . "The Chinese," says an Arab account of the ninth century, "makes from this horn girdles which fetch a price of two or three thousand dinars or more. . . ." The astonishing prices fetched by these horns and the intense delight taken by Chinese in ornaments made from them can hardly be explained by their rarity value alone: superstition as well as artistic taste must lie at the root of this passion. And indeed we find that "sometimes the horn is in the image of a man, or a peacock, or a fish or some other thing.*

DISTANT HILLS

For those men who passed the civil service examinations and accepted official posts, travel from place to place became a way of life. They were commonly transferred every three years. Su Shih was born in Szechwan near the foot of Mount Omei in 1037. Like many who rose to political and literary eminence in the Sung, he came from relatively humble people, "connected with the local weaving industry." His grandfather had been illiterate. He and his younger brother were locally tutored by a Daoist priest. Together with their father they travelled

*Gernet, pp. 131–2

the thousand-mile journey down the Yangtze and north to the capital of Kai-feng, where both boys passed the examinations the first try, a striking feat. In his early poem "On the Yangtze Watching the Hills"—travelling by boat with his father and brother through the San-hsia Gorge—Su Shih opens some of that space for us:

> From the boat watching hills—swift horses:
> a hundred herds race by in a flash.
> Ragged peaks before us suddenly change shape,
> Ranges behind us start and rush away.
> I look up: a narrow trail angles back and forth,
> A man walking it, high in the distance.
> I wave from the deck, trying to call,
> But the sail takes us south like a soaring bird.*

All three were given employment. In 1066 the father died and the two sons returned to bury him in Szechwan. It was the last time Su Shih saw his native village. He was 29.

This mobility contributes to the impression we get from Su and his cohorts that they no longer cared about

*Su Tung-P'o. *Selections from a Sung Dynasty Poet*, translated by Burton Watson (New York: Columbia University Press, 1965) p. 23

particular landscapes. Indeed, for many of them there was no place in China they called home enough to know the smells and the wild plants, but during their interminable journeys on river boats and canal barges the scenery slowly unrolled for them like a great scroll. At the same time there was a cheerful recognition and acceptance of the fact that "we live in society." The clear, dry funny poems of daily life with family and neighbors that came of this are marvelous. Daoist ideas of living in mountain isolation, or breaking conventions, came to be seen as romantic and irresponsible. Yoshikawa comments on the optimism of Sung poetry, and suggests that it echoes the optimism of the ancient *Book of Songs* (*Shih Ching*), with its care for daily tasks and the busy space within the farmyard. The dominant emotion expressed in T'ang dynasty writing is sorrow and grief: humankind is all too impermanent, only mountains and rivers will remain.* Sung poets like Mei Yao-ch'en might write in rough plain language, or a low-key style, of things the elegantly intense T'ang poets would never touch. Such is Yang Wan-li's poem on a fly:

*Kojiro Yoshikawa. *An Introduction to Sung Poetry*, translated by Burton Watson (Cambridge, MA: Harvard University Press, 1967) p. 25

Noted outside the window: a fly, the sun on his back,
rubbing his legs together, relishing the
    morning brightness.
Sun and shadow about to shift—already he
    knows it,
Suddenly flies off, to hum by a
    different window.*

Su Shih, lying on his back in a boat, takes detachment a
step further:

    I greet the breeze that happens along
  And lift a cup to offer to the vastness:
  How pleasant—that we have no thought of each
    other! †

Kojiro Yoshikawa's quick analysis of nature images in
Sung poetry notes that "sunset" is a common reference
in the T'ang with a strong overtone of sadness. Su Shih,
writing on a sunset seen from a Buddhist temple, is able
to freshly say

* Burton Watson. *Chinese Lyricism* (New York: Columbia University
Press, 1971) p. 202
† Yoshikawa, p. 23

Faint wind: on the broad water,
　　wrinkles like creases in a shoe;
Broken clouds: over half the sky,
　　a red the color of fish tails.*

　Rain, Yoshikawa observes, is a frequent Sung reference
— rain to listen to at night while talking with a bedmate,
rain to burn incense and study by.

　Shall I tell you the way to become a god
　　in this humdrum world?
　Burn some incense and sit listening to the rain.

LU YU†

In a society of such mobility, complexity, and size, it is
to be expected that a "sense of place" would be hard to
maintain. Humanistic concerns can be cultivated any-
where, but certain kinds of understanding and information about the natural world are only available to those
who stay put and keep looking. There is another kind
of "staying put" which flourished in some circles during
the Sung, namely the meditation practice of Ch'an Buddhism, *zazen*. What some Sung poets and thinkers may
have lost in terms of sense of natural place was balanced

*Yoshikawa, p. 47
†Yoshikawa, p. 48

perhaps by a better understanding of natural self. A different sort of grounding occurred.

Much of the distinctive quality of Sung poetry can be attributed to the influence of the relentless and original Su Shih. Su was also an advanced Ch'an practicer, which is evident in his resolute, penetrating, sensitive body of work. The Ch'an influence is not at its best in the poems about monks or temples; we find it in plainer places. But when Su says of the sky, "How pleasant—that we have no thought of each other" it is not to be taken as an expression of the heartlessness or remoteness of nature. Within the mutual mindlessness: of sky and self the Ch'an practicer enacts the vivid energy and form of each blade of grass, each pebble. The obsession that T'ang poets had with impermanence was a sentimental response to the commonly perceived stress of Mahayana Buddhism on transiency and evanescence. Ch'an teachers never bothered with self-pity, and brought a playful and courageous style of give-and-take to the study of impermanent phenomena. I suspect that Sung poets were more dyed with the true spirit of Ch'an than those of the T'ang. From the standpoint of the natural environment, the T'ang view can almost be reversed—it seems the mountains and rivers, or at least their forests and creatures, soils and beds, are more fragile than we thought. Human beings grimly endure.

THE BORE

The rulers and courtiers of Hang-chou never fully grasped the seriousness of the Mongol threat. Dallying in the parks, challenging each others' connoisseurship, they carried aestheticism to impressive levels. Mongka Khan, who ravaged Tibet, and his brother Khubla left Southern Sung on the back burner for a decade or so while they consolidated their northern and western borders.

In Hang-chou every September the people of the city thronged out to the banks of the Che River to witness a spectacle belonging to a scale even larger—their own unwitting point of contact with the dragons of the whole planetary water cycle. This was the annual high-point of the tidal bore which came in from the bay, up the river, and right by the town. Viewing platforms were erected for the emperor and his family. One year when the huge wall of water came rushing up, a surprise wind rose behind it, and the eagre went over the barriers and drowned hundreds of people.*

*Gernet, p. 195

MOUNT BURKHAN KHALDUN

Sung dynasty China was a high-water mark of civilization. Joseph Needham and Mark Elvin take thirteenth-century China to have been on the verge of a western-style technological revolution; at least many of the preconditions were there. (Yet it would be foolish to assume that such an evolution is necessarily desirable.) The Mongol conquest was a blow to the culture, but without it, China would probably have gone through a similar process—a stabilization, fading of innovation and experiment, and a long slow retreat of both economy and creativity. Having granted this decline, it must be pointed out that no Occidental culture can approach the time-scale of stability and relative prosperity this decline encompassed. Reischauer's comment that "there are few historic parallels except among primitive peoples"* strikes far.

Lively though it was, the Sung had severe problems. Half the people of the Northern Sung were tenant farmers paying half their farm income as rent to the landlords. Declining natural resources and growing population ended experimental ventures into labor-saving devices: materials grew expensive as labor became cheap. Smaller

---

*Reischauer and Fairbank, p. 241

farms, over-worked soil, and more people brought tax revenue and personal income down. The frontier territories of the south and southwest were saturated. In spite of all the (almost self-congratulatory) social concern of the Neo-Confucian philosophers, no analysis went deep enough. Millions of people who worked in the salt marshes of the Huai River valleys were virtual slaves.

Far north of the sinicized Juchen and their captured realm, across the Ordos and the Gobi, lived the Mongol tribes. Some Mongol groups associated Mount Burkhan Khaldun, near the head of the Onon River (a tributary of the Amur) and south-southeast of Lake Baikal, with their legendary ancestors the Blue Wolf and his wife the Fallow Deer. About 1185 an 18-year-old youth named Temujin fled for his life to the slopes of this mountain, pursued by rival Mongol horsemen of the Merkit tribe. For days they pursued him through the willow thickets and swamps of the densely forested upland. They could follow his horse's tracks but they could not catch up with him. Eventually the Merkit contented themselves with taking some women from the camps below, and left. *The Secret History of the Mongols* has Temujin saying, as he descends the mountain,

> Though it seemed that I'd be crushed like
>> a louse, I escaped to Mount
>> Burkhan Khaldun.
> The mountain has saved my life and my horse.
> Leading my horse down the elk-paths, making
>> my tent from the willow branches, I
>> went up Mount Burkhan.
> Though I was frightened and ran like an insect,
>> I was shielded by Mount Burkhan Khaldun.
> Every morning offer a sacrifice to
>> Mount Burkhan.
> Every day I'll pray to the mountains. Then
> striking his breast with his hand,
>> he knelt nine times to the sun. Sprinkling
> offerings of mare's milk in the air, And he
> prayed.*

This survivor, who had lived for years with his abandoned mother and brothers by trapping ground squirrels and marmots, snaring ducks, and fishing, went on to be chosen the supreme leader of all the Turko-Mongol tribes. At the gathering or *quriltai* of 1206 he was given the title

---

*Yuan Ch'ai Pi Shih. *Secret History of the Mongols*, translated by Paul Kahn (Berkeley: North Point Press, 1983)

"Jenghiz Khan." After that, he began his first campaign in northern China, attacking the cities of the Tungusic Chin. Many campaigns and victories later the Buddhist monk Li Chih-ch'ang visited him at his headquarters in Karakorum. Jenghiz Khan is reported as saying,

> Heaven is weary of the inordinate luxury of China. I remain in the wild region of the north, I return to simplicity and seek moderation once more. As for the garments that I wear and the meals that I eat, I have the same rags and the same food as cowherds and grooms, and I treat the soldiers as my brothers.*

Jenghiz Khan did not exactly live a simple life, but he was determined and very tough. He was also a brilliant military strategist. Many grassland nomad warriors before him had won victories from the Chinese or Turko-Iranians, but none left behind an empire and the beginnings of an administration. This was partly because he paid close attention to the engineers and architects among his prisoners of war, and they taught him how to besiege a city and how to broach the walls.

---

*Rene Grousset. *The Empire of the Steppes* (New Brunswick, NJ: Rutgers University Press, 1970) p. 249

Beyond Cathay: The Hill Tribes of China

The lands south of the Kiang (Yangtze) are broad and sparsely populated, and the people live on rice and fish soups. They burn off the fields and flood them to kill the weeds, and are able to gather all the fruit, berries, and univalve and bivalve shellfish they want without waiting for merchants to come around selling them. Since the land is so rich in edible products, there is no fear of famine, and therefore the people are content to live along from day to day: they do not lay away stores of goods, and many of them are poor. As a result, in the region south of the Yangtze and Huai rivers no one ever freezes or starves to death, but on the other hand there are no very wealthy families.

SSU-MA CHIEN, THE GRAND HISTORIAN
(D. 90 BC)

These people of the south, though the same race as the northern Chinese, were once considered barbarians, "monkeys with caps on." Now they are thoroughly assimilated, and most are fully accounted as civilized. Only in remote enclaves in the hills does some trace of the vast civilized southern Chinese world survive.

The source of the wealth of the Chinese state was the labor of the masses applied to cultivation of millet and rice. To the northeast of the northern Chinese heartlands (the lowlands along the Yellow River) the land climbs and the rainfall drops off. It is a high grassland and semidesert unsuited for agriculture. The south, difficult though it seemed, was convertible to agriculture up all the valleys and branches, so China expanded south. By 605 AD a grain transport canal system from the Yangtze north to the capital was completed, and southern China gradually began to become the most productive part of the empire. Over the centuries the lowland-dwelling natives were converted to Chinese ways, their Chinese names put on the tax lists, and the ethnic past forgotten, or Hua (the old term for heartland Chinese) immigrants simply overwhelmed them with their numbers. However, the specialized agricultural system that was so appropriated in the lowlands had less economic use for the hills. Hundreds of upland islands of non-Hua culture survived as scattered forest communities in which hunting and gathering was combined with slash-and-burn farming. They did not give up easily; within the area of Hupei-

Shensi-Honan-Anhwei, the very center, there were over forty insurrections of tribal peoples between 404 AD and 561 AD. South of the Kiang, or Yangtze, watershed and west in Kweichow and Yunnan there are some very large populations that are mostly non-Chinese, known nowadays by such names as Yi, Pai, Tai, Miao, Yao, and Lisu.

Much of this southern landscape is over three thousand feet high and rises in western Yunnan and Szechwan as high as fifteen thousand feet. The southeastern part has the heaviest rainfall in all China—as much as ninety inches a year on the hills. In Keichow, the main home of the Miao people, the protected forest of Wumong Mountain gives us a sample of what the southwestern forest was all once like: walnuts, alders, dogwoods, tulip trees, liquidamber, beech, evergreen, oak, chinquapins, and members of the laurel family such as cinnamon and sassafras. Outside such protected areas the later successional pines are now dominant.

In Tang and Sung times the non-Hua peoples of the south were collectively called the Man, the "Man" of Marco Polo's "Manzi," the area in his travels south of what he calls "Cathay." *Man* is the word translated into English as "barbarian." The oldest name for the area, in Medieval Chinese pronunciation, is Nam-Ywat, which in modern Mandarin is Nan-Yueh—"South Yueh"—and in another modern pronunciation (the "south" reversed) "Vietnam." In the politics of Tang times this southern region included the whole southern Chinese coast, and the major city was Canton; the territorial boundary was south of the delta of the Red River, south of Hanoi, where Chinese cultural influence was finally brought up against the cultural influence of India—the Cham empire. *Ywat* probably means "ax"; the southerners were people of the "stone ax." In Vietnam the surviving hill tribes, essentially of the same lineages as those farther north, are now called "montagnards." These many peoples speak languages of the Sino-Tibetan family: Tibetan, Burman, Tai, Yao, and Miao. The tribes were called Huang, Nung, Mak, La, Ning, Lao. On the southwestern border of Yunan a few peoples spoke a Mon-Khmer language.

Travelling through the south in the thirteenth century, Marco Polo writes of the freedom of the women and constant rumors of violence and brigandage. Some of this may have been heard from prudish and patriarchal Chinese. He describes a rich life: "The traveller enters a country of great mountains and valleys and forests, through which he makes his way for twenty days towards the west. . . . The people are idolators, living on the fruits of the earth, on wild game and domestic animals. There are lions, bears, and lynxes, harts, stags, and roebuck, besides great numbers of the little deer that produce musk." (It seems unlikely he saw lions.)

The Hua people regarded the tribal Man as semi-animals, whose speech resembled the chatter of monkeys. There was a totemic legend of a dog ancestor among the Miao, the Nosu, or Lolo, now called Yi by the Peoples' Republic that had a "pine tree ancestor." Such legends only confirmed this view for the conquerors. Yet the Hua found the Man women beautiful. There was a regular trade in girls of the southern tribes who were sold as concubine-slaves to wealthy Chinese of the north. The fighting courage of the men was also acknowledged — "They love swords, and treat death lightly." The Chinese scorned them for their occasional cannibalism and head-hunting and then sent against them the sadistic general Yang Szu-hsu, who built a pyramid of the bodies of natives he killed in 722 AD and reputedly took scalps and peeled the skin from the faces of prisoners.

In spite of uprisings and struggle there were also periods of peaceful trade between the tribesmen and the Chinese. The government policy of "controlling barbarians with barbarians" meant sanctioning the authority of some chiefs over others, and in return receiving tribute: kingfisher feathers, elephant tusks, and rhinoceros horn. In China, as in North America and Siberia, when natural peoples get caught in a trade relationship with a civilization, it is the wildlife which suffers first.

Liu Yu-hsi was exiled in Kwangtung in the ninth century. Edward Schafer translates his "Song of the Man":

> The speech of the Man is a *kou-chou* sound. The
> dress of the Man is a *pan-lan* linen. Their odorous
> raccoons dig out the sand rats; At seasonal periods
> they sacrifice to P'an-hu. Should they meet a stranger
> riding a horse, They are flustered, and glance round
> like
> > startled muntjacs.
> With axes at their waists they ascend the high
> > mountains,
> Proposing to go where no old road exists.

Assimilated Man individuals were scarcely distinguishable from Hua Chinese, and some rose to local power as merchants or administrators. Perhaps the most famous aboriginal half-breed in Chinese history is the sixth patriarch of the Ch'an sect, Hui-nêng. Hui-nêng's father was Hua, but his mother was an aboriginal—possibly a Lao. His biography apologetically says, "Although he was soaked and dyed with the airs of the Man and the customs of the Lao, they were not deep in him." According to one legend, Bodhidharma himself came into China by way of the southern port of Canton. (In the territory of the Miao nation, now called Kweichow, early Buddhists carved images on the cliffs in the southern style of Javanese and South Indian art.) The "Southern School" of Ch'an, which may have started with Hui-nêng, is notorious for its vivid rejection of received forms and ideas and its demand that we look directly into the ground of Mind without preconceptions. Perhaps the earthy and independent lives of the indigenous peoples, through Hui-nêng, contributed to the force and flavor of this still flourishing school of Ch'an/Zen.

The most prized of all incenses used in the temples of the Far Eastern Buddhist world is from resinous aloe wood, called *jinko* in Japanese. Its smoke pervades the high-ceilinged head temples at Founders Day ceremonies in Kyoto even today. It was obtained in trade with the isolated aboriginal Li people of Hainan, who got steel axes, cereals, silks, and hatchets in return.

Today, the People's Republic of China had made almost half of Kweichow province, where three million Miao are living, into an autonomous district. The whole province of Kwangsi, home of seven million Tai-speaking Chuang, is also autonomous. Yunnan has a number of autonomous districts for the Tibet-Burman hill people. Mainstream

Chinese and Christian missionaries alike have been jolted by the Miao. An American traveler of the twenties wrote: "Every village had its club-house where the girls gathered nightly to sing and dance, and where the youths not of their own but from neighboring villages came to try them out as possible wives." The women wore brilliant multi-colored blouses, jackets, and skirts—"red perhaps pre-dominating in the intricate patterns, but no conceivable combination of colors barred. Evidently there was noth-ing worn beneath the short, pleated skirts that swung so saucily as the girls walked . . . cut so conveniently for hoeing corn on a steep hillside."* The Miao distilled their own alcohol and had a supposedly spectacular orgiastic festival, called "Fifth of the Fifth," up until recently.

It is significant that the mountain forests, much altered in the past few centuries, were protected and replanted more by the local mountain people than by the economi-cally dominant Chinese, at least before the PRC took over. The way the tribes saw their wild hills as home, and the wildlife as fellow beings, is apparent in their magical folklore term for the tiger: in myths and tales he is called "Streaked Lad."

Harry A. Franck. *Roving Through Southern China* (New York: Century, 1925) p. 494

Wolf-Hair Brush

The elites of premodern China's high civilization were urbane, bookish, secular, arty, and supremely confident. The Imperial Government rested in a ritualized relationship with Great Nature, and the seasonal exchanges between Heaven and Earth—sun, rains, and soils—were national sacraments conducted at elaborate Earth and Heaven shrines. (The most powerful of rituals were conducted in solitude by the Emperor himself.)

Nature and its landscapes were seen as realms of purity and selfless beauty and order, in vivid contrast to the corrupt and often brutal entanglements of politics that no active Chinese official could avoid. The price an intellectual paid for the prestige and affluence that came with being a member of the elite was the sure knowledge of the gap between humane Confucian theory and the actual practices of administering a county or a province—with multiple levels of graft, well-cooked books, and subtle techniques of coercion. And the higher one rose in the ranks, the more one's neck was exposed to the deadly intrigues of enemies.

The mountain horizons were a reminder of the vivid world of clear water, patient rocks, intensely focused trees, lively coiling clouds and mists — all the spontaneous processes that seemed to soar above human fickleness. The fu (prose-poem) poet Sun Ch'o said of these processes, "When the Dao dissolves, it becomes rivers, when it coagulates it becomes mountains." Tsung Ping, an early fifth-century painter whose work does not survive, is described has having done mountain landscapes when ill and no longer able to ramble the hills he loved. He wrote the perfect program for a recluse:

> Thus by living leisurely, by controlling the vital breath, by wiping the goblet, by playing the *ch'in*, by contemplating pictures in silence, by meditating on the four quarters of space, by never resisting the influence of Heaven and by responding to the call of the wilderness where the cliffs and peaks rise to dazzling heights and the cloudy forests are dense and vast, the wise and virtuous men of ancient times found innumerable pleasures which they assimilated by their souls and minds.*

* Quoted in Oswald Siren. *The Chinese on the Art of Painting* (New York: Schocken, 1963) p. 16

He also stated a philosophy of landscape painting that stood for centuries to come: "Landscapes exist in the material world yet soar in the realms of the spirit ... the Saint interprets the Way as Law through his spiritual insight, and so the wise man comes to an understanding of it. Landscape pays homage to the Way through Form, and so the virtuous man comes to delight in it."* Half a century later Hsieh Ho declared the First Principle of landscape painting to be "Spirit resonance and living moment"—meaning, a good painting is one in which the very rocks come alive, and one yearns to go walking in it. The basic aesthetics of the tradition had been articulated, but it was almost a thousand years before the implications of these statements were fully realized in painterly terms. The art of painting "mountains and waters" slowly unfolded through the centuries.

The concept of *ch'i*—a term that translates as indwelling energy, breath, and spirit—is a rich sophistication of archaic East Asian animism. Joseph Needham calls it "matter-energy" and treats it as a proto-scientific term. Contemporary people everywhere tend to see matter as lifeless. The notion of a rock participating in life and

*Quoted in J. L. Frodsham. *The Murmuring Stream*, Vol I (Kuala Lumpur: U. of Malaya, 1976) p. 103

spirit — even as metaphor — is beneath adult consideration. Yet for those who work for long amid the forms of nature, the resonating presence of a river-system or prairie expanse or range of hills becomes faintly perceptible. It's odd but true that if too much human impact has hit the scene, this presence doesn't easily rise.

Archaic art worldwide is often abstract and geometrical. The spiral motif is widely found — from tattoos on the cheek to petroglyphs on a canyon wall. This representation of the *ch'i* of things becomes a design of volutes in very early Chinese decorative art. Artists started tracing the lines of energy flow as observed in the clouds, running water, mist and rising smoke, plant growth — tendrils, rock formations, and various effects of light, in their patterns. They went on, according to Michael Sullivan, to draw images of fantastically-formed animal/energy-bodied nature spirits, and this provided a main bridge from archetypal being to archetypal landform. The lines finally twisted themselves into ranges of mountains.*

The word for civilization in Chinese is *wên-ming*, literally, "understanding writing." In the time of Confucius

---

* Michael Sullivan. "On the Origins of Landscape Representation in Chinese Art." Archives of the Chinese Art Society of America VII, 1953, pp. 61–62

people wrote on slats of bamboo with a stylus. When paper and the soft-haired brush came into use, the fluidity of calligraphy became possible. In China calligraphy is considered the highest of the graphic arts. The painter uses the same equipment as a writer—the "four treasures" of brush, ink, inkstone, and paper. The brush usually has a bamboo handle with rabbit, badger, goat, deer, wolf, sable, fox, and other hairs for the tip. Even mouse-whiskers have been tried. Everything from a broken roof-tile to rare and unusual stones have been used for grinding the ink. Paper, which is said to have been invented in the first century AD, is commonly made from mulberry, hemp, and bamboo. The paper preferred by Sung and Yuan dynasty painters was called "Pure Heart Hall" paper. It was smooth, white, and thin. Paintings were also done on silk, but paper lasts longer. Ink was made by burning dry pine logs in a kind of soot-collecting kiln. The soot was mixed with glue, one famous glue being made of donkey skin boiled in water from the Tung River. Fragrance was added, and the whole pressed into an inscribed stick.* Grinding the ink with a slow steady back-and-forth stroke, softening the brush, spreading the

*Sze Mai Mai. *The Way of Chinese Landscape Painting* (New York: Vintage, 1959)

paper — amounts to a meditation on the qualities of rock, water, trees, air, and shrubs.

The earliest surviving landscape paintings (early T'ang, the seventh century) are more like perspective maps. Wang Wei's *Wang Chuan Villa* is a visual guide to a real place, with little labels on the notable locations. These first painted mountains are stark and centered, and the trees look stuck on. The painting might be a guide-book scene of a famous temple on a famous mountain. They are still half-tied to accounts of journeys, land-use records, or poems.

Then, with the Sung dynasty, the eleventh century, paintings open out to great space. The rock formations, plants and trees, river and stream systems, flow through magically realistic spatial transitions. The painter-essayist Kuo Hsi reminded us that the mountains change their appearance at every step you take. For those interested in bio-geographic provinces the paintings can be seen to be distinguishing the wider drier mountains of the north from the tighter, wetter, mistier valleys of the south. These vast scenes, with a few small fishing boats, little huts — cottages — travellers with pack stock — become visionary timeless lands of mountain-rocks and air-mist-breath and far calm vistas. People are small but are lovingly rendered, doing righteous tasks or reclining and enjoying their world.

In terms of technique painters moved between extremes of wet ink-dripping brushes and drier sparser ink on the brush. From hard-boned fine-detailed meticulous workmanship leaf by leaf and pebble by pebble it went to wet flung washes of lights and darks that capture a close hill, a distant range, a bank of trees with an effect that can be called impressionistic.

The Sung dynasty painters of large scale, including the horizontal handscrolls of a type sometimes called "Streams and Mountains Without End," didn't always walk the hills they portrayed. With an established vocabulary of forms and the freedom of the brush they could summon up mountains that totally defied gravity and geomorphology, and seemed to float in mist. But these invented landscapes were somehow true to organic life and the energy-cycles of the biosphere. The paintings show us the earth surface as part of a living being, on which water, cloud, rock, and plant growth all stream through each other—the rocks under water, waterfalls coming down from above clouds, trees flourishing in air. I overstate to make the point: the cycles of biosphere process do just this, stream vertically through each other. The swirls and spirals of micro- and macroclimate ("the tropical heat engine" for example) are all creations of living organisms; the whole atmosphere is a breath of plants, writhing over the planet in elegant feedback coils instructed by thermodynamics and whatever it is that guides complexity. "Nature by self-entanglement produces beauty." *

The mountains and rivers of the Sung dynasty paintings are numinous and remote. Yet they could be walked. Climbers take pleasure in gazing on ranges from a near distance and visualizing the ways to approach and ascend. Faces that seem perpendicular from afar are in fact not, and impossible-looking foreshortened spur-ridges or gullies have slopes, notches, ledges, that one can negotiate — a trained eye can see them. Studying Fan K'uan's "Travellers Among Streams and Mountains" (about 1000 AD) — a hanging scroll seven feet tall — one can discern a possible climbing route up the chimneys to the left of the waterfall. The travellers and their packstock are safe below on the trail. They could be coming into the Yosemite Valley in the 1870s.† Southern Sung and Yuan dynasty landscape painting (especially with the horizontal handscroll format) tends to soften the hills. In the time

---

* Otto Rössler, quoted in Gleick. *Chaos* (Penguin, 1987) p. 142
† Fan K'uan's painting can be seen in plate 11 in Wen Fong. *Summer Mountains* (New York Metropolitan Museum of Art, 1975). Original is in the National Palace Museum, Taipei. Also in Lee and Fong [see footnote on page 127 for full citation], plate 8.

of the evolution of the paintings, the mountains become easier, and finally can be easily rambled from one end to the other. As Sherman Lee says the landscapes are no longer "mountain- and-water" but "rock-and-tree-and-water."*

The cities of the lower Yangtze became a haven for refugee artists and scholars during the Southern Sung dynasty, twelfth century, when the northern half of the country fell to the Khitans, a forest-dwelling Mongol tribe from Manchuria. The long-established southern intelligentsia had always been closer to Daoism than the northerners. At that time Ch'an Buddhism and painting both were popularly divided into a northern and southern school. In both cases, the southern school was taken to be more immediate and intuitive. This large community of artists in the south launched new styles of painting. Lighter, more intimate, suggestive, swift, and also more realistic. Some of the painters—Hsia Kuei, Mu Ch'i, Liang K'ai—were much admired by the Japanese Zen monks and merchants, so many of their works were bought by the Japanese, traded for the exquisite Japanese swords that the Chinese needed to fight off the northern

*Sherman E. Lee and Wen Fong. *Streams and Mountains Without End* (Ascona, Switzerland: Artibus Asiae, 1976) p. 19

invaders. Many of the paintings ended up in the Zen Honzans ("Main Mountains"—headquarters temples) of Kyoto, where they are kept today.

The fact that some scrolls were landscapes of the imagination should not be allowed to obscure the achievement of Chinese artists in rendering actual landscapes. The most fantastic-looking peaks of the scrolls have models in the karst limestone pinnacles of Kuangsi; misty cliffs and clinging pines are characteristic of the ranges of southern Anhwei province. The painting manual *Chieh-tzu Yuan Hua Chuan*, "Mustard-seed Garden Guide to Painting" (about 1679) distinguishes numerous types of mountain formations, and provides a traditional menu of appropriate brushstroke-types for evoking them. Geological identifications of the forms indicated by different brushstrokes are described in Needham: "Glaciated or maturely eroded slopes, sometimes steep, are shown by the technique called 'spread-out hemp fibers,' and mountain slopes furrowed by water into gullies are drawn in the *ho yeh ts'un* manner ('veins of a lotus-leaf hung up to dry'). 'Unraveled rope' indicates igneous intrusions and granite peaks; 'rolling clouds' suggest fantastically contorted eroded schists. The smooth roundness of exfoliated igneous rocks is seen in the 'bullock hair' method, irregularly jointed and slightly weathered granite appears in 'broken nets', and extreme erosion gives 'devil face' or 'skull' forms . . . cleavages across strata, with vertical jointed up-right angular rocks, looking somewhat like crystals, are depicted in the 'horse teeth' (*ma ya ts'un*) technique." *

The *Ta Ch'ing I Tung Chih* is an eighteenth-century geographical encyclopedia with an illustrated chapter on "mountains and rivers." These woodblocks, based on the painting tradition, not only give a fair rendering of specific scenes, but do so with geological precision. Needham notes how one can identify water-rounded boulder deposits, the Permian basalt cliffs of Omei-shan, the dipping strata of the Hsiang mountains near Po tomb, U-shaped valleys and rejuvenated valleys.†

Huang Kung-wang (born in 1269) was raised in the south. After a short spell with the civil service he became a Daoist teacher, poet, musician, and painter. He is said to have recommended that one should "carry around a sketching brush in a leather bag" and called out to his students "look at the clouds—they have the appearance of mountain tops!" †† His handscroll "Dwelling in the

*Joseph Needham. *Science and Civilization in China III*. p. 597
† Ibid., pp. 593-7
††James Cahill. *Hills Beyond a River* (New York: Weatherhill, 1976).

Fu-ch'un Mountains" * came to be one of the most famous paintings within China. He started it one summer afternoon in 1347, looking out from his house, and doing the whole basic composition on that one day. It took another three years to finish it. It's a clean, graceful painting that breathes a spirit of unmystified naturalness. The scene is not particularly wild or glamorous; it has the plain power of simply being its own quite recognizable place. This is in tune with the Ch'an demand for "nothing special" and its tenderness for every entity, however humble.

From around the Ming dynasty (1368 on) China had more and more people living in the cities. Painting helped keep a love of wild nature alive, but it gradually came to be that many paintings were done by people who had never much walked the hills, for clients who would never get a chance to see such places. There were also later painters like Wang Hui, who was a master of all historical styles, but also an acute observer of nature. His "Landscape in the Style of Chü-jan and Yen Wen-Kuei" (1713) carries the hills and slopes on out to sea as the painting fades away, by a portrayal of sea-fog twisting into scrolls and curls of water-vapor / wind-current / energy-flow that

---

* Ibid. Plates 41–44; Color Plate 5. Original is in the National Palace Museum in Taipei.

faintly reminds us of the origins of Chinese paintings, and takes us back to the mineral- and water-cycle sources. Chinese painting never strays far from its grounding in energy, life, and process.

The space goes on.
But the wet black brush
tip drawn to a point,
        lifts away.